MW01283189

BOOK RICH

How to Create a Fortune as a
Self-Published Author

ASH CASH EXANTUS

DISCLAIMER

The advice contained in this material might not be suitable for everyone. The author designed the information to present his opinion about the subject matter. The reader must carefully investigate all aspects of any business decision before committing to him or herself. The author obtained the information contained herein from sources he believes to be reliable and from his own personal experience, but he neither implies nor intends any guarantee of accuracy. The author is not in the business of giving legal, accounting, or any other type of professional advice. Should the reader need such advice, he or she must seek services from a competent professional. The author particularly disclaims any liability, loss, or risk taken by individuals who directly or indirectly act on the information contained herein. The author believes the advice presented here is sound, but readers cannot hold him responsible for either the actions they take, or the risk taken by individuals who directly or indirectly act on the information contained herein.

Published by 1BrickPublishing
Printed in the United States
Copyright © 2023 by Ash'Cash
ISBN 978-1949303407

DEDICATION

This book is dedicated to anyone who has a story and/or a business and is looking for ways to turn that story into income and impact! To those who have a business and want to build multiple streams of income around that business and to those who know that their story can save someone's life.

DEDICATION REQUEST

Please pass a copy of this book to anyone you care about who needs some inspiration, motivation, and practical tips on how to build a lasting legacy and share their story with the world!

TABLE OF CONTENTS

Chapter IV

Marketing and Promotion....................................159

Chapter V

Scaling Your Success 167

Chapter VI

INTRODUCTION

Welcome to "Book Rich: How to Create a Fortune as a Self-Published Author." In this book, we will explore the world of self-publishing and how any entrepreneur or business owner can add an additional 6-Figures or more to their business with a book they don't even have to write. The self-publishing industry has grown exponentially in recent years, and the opportunities for authors to make a living from their writing have never been greater.

But it's not just about writing and publishing a book, it's about creating multiple streams of income from your book. In this book, we will cover all aspects of self-publishing, from choosing a profitable niche and building a platform to crafting a compelling book idea, formatting and designing your book, and publishing and distribution options. We will also delve into monetizing your book through traditional book sales, royalties, and rights, and leveraging it for other income streams.

We will also cover essential topics such as building a marketing plan, utilizing social media, networking, and partnerships, and book launches and events. And we will also cover the importance of scaling your success by writing multiple books, building a brand, outsourcing, and delegation, and staying current in the industry.

By the end of this book, you will have the knowledge and tools to turn your passion into a profitable career as a self-published author. You'll be able to create financial freedom and build a personal fortune through writing and publishing.

Before we begin our journey to becoming a "Book Rich" author let's discuss why now is a great time for entrepreneurs and business owners to become authors or why current authors need to rethink their business model and strategy. The self-publishing industry has grown significantly in recent years, with more and more authors choosing to self-publish their work. This growth is driven by advances in technology and the rise of digital platforms, which have made self-publishing easier and more accessible than ever before.

Self-publishing allows authors to retain full control over their work, from the writing and editing process to the design and formatting of their book. It also enables authors to bypass the traditional gatekeepers of the publishing industry, such as literary agents and traditional publishers.

Authors can choose from a variety of self-publishing options, such as e-book publishing, print-on-demand, and vanity publishing. E-book publishing, in particular, has become increasingly popular as it allows authors to reach a global audience and eliminates the need for a large initial print run.

The self-publishing industry is also becoming more competitive, with more authors self-publishing their work. This means that authors need to be more strategic in their approach to self-publishing, focusing on building a platform, creating a strong brand, and effectively marketing their book.

The rise of self-publishing has also led to the emergence of new business models, such as hybrid publishing, where authors can benefit from the support and services of a traditional publisher, while maintaining control over their work.

Overall, the self-publishing industry has grown in complexity and diversity, and it is becoming a viable alternative to traditional publishing. It is providing more opportunities for authors to reach readers and make a living from their writing. Also, with the advancement of technology creating multiple streams of income from books has become easier and in today's economic environment multiple streams of income has become extremely important.

Creating multiple streams of income is important for a variety of reasons. One of the main benefits is that it helps to diversify your income, which can provide a safety net in case one of your income streams dries up.

For example, if you rely on a single stream of income from your book sales, you may find that your income is unstable and unpredictable. However, if you have multiple streams of income, such as royalties, speaking engagements, coaching, or consulting, you are likely to be less affected if your book sales decline.

Another benefit of creating multiple streams of income is that it can help you to increase your overall income. By diversifying your income, you can tap into different markets and revenue sources, which can help you to increase your earning potential.

Additionally, creating multiple streams of income can also provide you with a sense of security and peace of mind. Knowing that you have multiple sources of income can help you to feel more financially secure and less dependent on any one source of income.

In the context of self-publishing, creating multiple streams of income can be particularly important. Self-publishing is a competitive industry and relying solely on book sales can be risky. By creating multiple streams of income, self-published authors can increase their earning potential and reduce their dependence on book sales.

Overall, creating multiple streams of income is an important strategy for anyone looking to build financial stability and increase their earning potential. It is a key aspect of becoming "Book Rich" as a self-published author.

Before diving into the strategies and techniques outlined in this book, it's important to understand the potential of self-publishing as a means to not only create multiple streams of income, but also to establish a lasting legacy. Books can be a powerful asset in achieving both of these goals.

As we have discussed, creating multiple streams of income is crucial for financial stability and growth. Self-publishing can provide a variety of opportunities for authors to monetize their work and diversify their income. By leveraging the credibility and expertise gained from publishing a book, authors can expand into related fields such as speaking engagements, coaching, and consulting, as well as develop book-based businesses.

Additionally, a book can serve as a lasting legacy, preserving your knowledge and ideas for future generations. The examples of Napoleon Hill, Stephen Covey, and Dr. Seuss who are all deceased authors whose books are currently bestsellers on many platforms demonstrate the potential for books to continue generating income and impacting lives long after the author's death.

It's important to take the self-publishing process seriously and to follow the strategies outlined in this book. By doing so, you can not only create multiple streams of income, but also establish a lasting legacy through your written work. So, let's begin our journey to becoming a "Book Rich" author!

CHAPTER I

SETTING YOURSELF UP FOR SUCCESS

Setting yourself up for success as a self-published author involves a few key steps that will help you to create a strong foundation for your book and your career.

1. Choosing a Profitable Niche: Before you start writing, it's essential to choose a niche that has a profitable market. It's important to research the competition, understand the target audience, and identify the specific problem that your book will solve.

2. Building a Platform and Audience: Having a platform and an audience is crucial to the success of your book. Building a platform involves creating a website, starting a blog, and building a presence on social media. Building an audience involves engaging with potential readers, providing valuable content, and building relationships.

3. Understanding the Business Side of Self-publishing: Self-publishing is not just about writing, it's also about the business side of things. Understanding the business side of self-publishing

involves understanding the different types of self-publishing options available, understanding how to format and design your book, and understanding how to market and promote your book.

By following these steps, you will be setting yourself up for success as a self-published author. You will be able to create a strong foundation for your book, your platform, and your audience, and will be able to make well-informed decisions about the business side of self-publishing.

Choosing a Profitable Niche

Choosing a profitable niche is an important step in setting yourself up for success as a self-published author. A profitable niche is a specific market or topic that has a high demand for books and low competition.

When choosing a niche, it's important to research and understand the target audience. Who are they? What are their needs, wants, and pain points? What kind of books are they currently reading? By understanding your target audience, you'll be able to create a book that speaks directly to them and their needs.

It's also important to research the competition in your chosen niche. What kind of books are already available? What are the bestsellers in that niche? What are the gaps in the market? By understanding the competition, you'll be able to create a book that stands out and fills a gap in the market.

It's also important to identify the specific problem that your book will solve. What unique knowledge, insights, or information will your book provide? How will it add value to the readers' lives? By answering these questions, you'll be able to create a book that has a clear purpose and will be in high demand.

Lastly, it's also important to consider the earning potential in your niche. Are there opportunities for royalties, rights, and other income streams beyond book sales? Is there a potential for a book-based business?

Choosing a profitable niche is an important step in setting yourself up for success as a self-published author. By researching your target audience, understanding the competition, identifying the specific problem that your book will solve, and considering the earning potential, you'll be able to choose a niche that has a high demand and low competition, which will increase your chances of success.

BUILDING A PLATFORM AND AUDIENCE

Building a platform and audience is crucial to the success of your book as a self-published author. A platform is a way for you to connect with potential readers, promote your book, and build your brand. An audience is a group of people who are interested in your book and are likely to buy it.

Here are a few ways to build a platform and audience:

1. Create a website: A website is a central hub for all of your online activities. It's a place where people can learn more about you, your book, and your brand.

2. Start a blog: A blog is a great way to connect with your audience and provide valuable content. It's also a way to establish yourself as an expert in your field.

3. Build a presence on social media: social media is a great way to connect with potential readers, promote your book, and build your brand. It's important to choose the platforms that your target audience is most active on.

4. Engage with your audience: Engage with your audience by responding to comments and messages, and by creating a sense of community. This will help to build trust and loyalty.

5. Provide value: Provide value to your audience by sharing helpful information and resources. This will help to establish you as an expert and make people more likely to buy your book.

6. Network and Partner: Networking and partnerships can help you to reach new audiences and expand your platform.

Building a platform and audience takes time and effort, but it's essential for the success of your book. By creating a website, starting a blog, building a presence on social media, engaging with your audience, providing value, and networking, you'll be able to connect with potential readers, promote your book, and build your brand.

Understanding the Business Side of Self-Publishing

Understanding the business side of self-publishing is an important step in setting yourself up for success as a self-published author. It involves understanding the different types of self-publishing options available, understanding how to format and design your book, and understanding how to market and promote your book.

1. Types of self-publishing options: There are various self-publishing options available, such as e-book publishing, print-on-demand, and vanity publishing. Each option has its own pros and cons, and it's important to understand which one is best for your book and your goals.

2. Formatting and Designing your book: Proper formatting and design can make a huge difference in the perceived value of your book. It's important to understand the basics of book layout, typography, and cover design.

3. Marketing and Promotion: Marketing and promotion are essential for the success of your book. You need to understand the different ways to market and promote your book, such as social media, book reviews, book signings, and giveaways.

4. Pricing and Distribution: It's important to understand the pricing strategies, distribution channels and the costs associated with them. This will help you to make informed decisions about how to price and distribute your book.

5. Royalties and Rights: Understanding royalties and rights is important for authors looking to monetize their book. It's

important to understand what royalties are, how they are calculated, and how to protect your rights.

By understanding the business side of self-publishing, you'll be able to make informed decisions about how to publish, format, design, market, promote, price and distribute your book. This will help you to increase your chances of success as a self-published author. To learn how to properly execute all of the above make sure you check out **BookRichUniversity.com** or use our software at **BookRich.io**

CHAPTER II

Writing and Publishing Your Book

Writing and publishing your book is the final step in the process of becoming a self-published author. This step involves completing the actual writing of your book and making it available to readers through various publishing and distribution channels. Here are a few key elements to consider:

1. Writing your book: The actual process of writing your book will vary depending on your writing style and the type of book you are writing. It's important to set a schedule for yourself and to stick to it.

2. Editing and proofreading: Once your book is written, it's important to have it professionally edited and proofread. This will ensure that your book is free of errors and is of the highest quality.

3. Formatting and Designing: Once your book is written and edited, you'll need to format and design it in a way that will make it appealing to readers.

4. Publishing: There are different ways to publish your book such as e-book, print-on-demand, and vanity publishing. Each one has its own pros and cons, and it's important to choose the one that best suits your book and your goals.

5. Distribution: Once your book is published, it's important to distribute it to the right channels. This includes online retailers such as Amazon, Barnes & Noble, and Apple Books, as well as physical bookstores.

6. Marketing and Promotion: After your book is published, it's important to market and promote it so that potential readers can find it. This includes creating a book launch plan, utilizing social media, and reaching out to book reviewers.

Writing and publishing your book is the final step in the process of becoming a self-published author. By following these steps, you'll be able to ensure that your book is of the highest quality, is published in the right way, and is made available to readers through various channels.

Crafting a Compelling Book Idea

Crafting a compelling book idea is an essential step in the process of writing and publishing a book. A compelling book idea is one that is unique, interesting, and has the potential to capture the attention of a wide range of readers. Here are a few steps to help you craft a compelling book idea:

1. Identify your target audience: Before you start crafting your book idea, it's essential to identify your target audience. Who are they? What are their needs, wants, and pain points? What kind of books are they currently reading? By understanding your target audience, you'll be able to create a book that speaks directly to them.

2. Research the market: Research the market to understand the competition and the gaps in the market. What are the bestsellers in your niche? What are the gaps in the market? By understanding the competition, you'll be able to create a book that stands out and fills a gap in the market.

3. Identify the problem: Identify the specific problem that your book will solve. What unique knowledge, insights, or information will your book provide? How will it add value to the readers' lives? By answering these questions, you'll be able to create a book that has a clear purpose and will be in high demand.

4. Create an angle: Create an angle that makes your book unique and interesting. This could be a new perspective, a different approach or a new way of looking at a subject.

5. Test your idea: Test your idea by sharing it with others and getting feedback. Use this feedback to refine your idea and make sure it resonates with your target audience.

By following these steps, you'll be able to craft a compelling book idea that is unique, interesting, and has the potential to capture the attention of a wide range of readers. This will increase your chances of success as a self-published author.

WRITING AND EDITING TIPS

Writing and editing are important steps in the process of creating a successful book. Here are some tips to help you write and edit your book effectively:

1. Set a writing schedule: Set a writing schedule and stick to it. This will help you to stay focused and motivated and to make steady progress on your book.

2. Eliminate distractions: Eliminate distractions while you're writing, such as social media, email, and phone notifications.

3. Write in a comfortable environment: Write in a comfortable environment that is conducive to your writing process. This could be a quiet room, a cozy coffee shop, or a park bench.

4. Write in chunks: Break your writing into chunks, such as writing for an hour at a time. This will help you to stay focused and to make steady progress.

5. Write first, edit later: When you're writing, focus on getting your thoughts down on paper without worrying about editing. Save the editing for later.

6. Use a thesaurus: Use a thesaurus to find new and interesting words to add to your writing.

7. Read your work aloud: Read your work aloud to help you catch mistakes and to get a sense of how your writing sounds to the reader.

8. Get feedback: Get feedback from others, such as beta readers, to help you improve your writing and to identify areas that need editing.

9. Take breaks: Taking breaks is important to let your mind rest and to avoid burnout.

By following these tips, you'll be able to write and edit your book effectively and increase your chances of creating a successful book.

If you are busy like most entrepreneurs and business owners, you may not have time to actually write your book so you may want to consider dictating your book.

Here are a few steps to help you get started:

1. Prepare your equipment: To dictate your book, you'll need a device that can record audio, such as a smartphone, tablet, or digital recorder. It's also a good idea to invest in a high-quality microphone to improve the audio quality.
2. Create an outline: Before you start dictating, it's important to create an outline for your book. This will help you to stay organized and keep your thoughts on track.
3. Find a quiet place: Make sure to find a quiet place to dictate your book, away from any background noise that might disrupt your recording.
4. Speak clearly: Speak clearly and at a moderate pace. Make sure to pause between thoughts and to enunciate your words.
5. Dictate in short bursts: Dictating in short bursts is a good way to avoid fatigue and to ensure that you're speaking clearly. Take breaks as needed.

6. Transcribe the audio: Once you have finished dictating, you'll need to transcribe the audio into written text. You can do this yourself or hire a transcriptionist to do it for you.

7. Edit and proofread: Once you have transcribed the audio, you'll need to edit and proofread your book to ensure that it's free of errors and is of the highest quality.

Dictating a book can be a great option for authors who prefer to speak their ideas rather than writing them. By following these steps, you'll be able to effectively dictate your book, transcribe the audio, and prepare it for publishing.

FORMATTING AND DESIGNING YOUR BOOK

Formatting and designing your book is an important step in the process of self-publishing. Proper formatting and design can make a huge difference in the perceived value of your book and it's important to understand the basics of book layout, typography, and cover design. Here are a few tips to help you format and design your book effectively:

1. Understand book layout: Understand the basic layout of a book, such as margins, page numbers, and chapter headings. This will ensure that your book looks professional.

2. Choose the right font: Choose a font that is easy to read and that is appropriate for the genre of your book.

3. Pay attention to typography: Pay attention to the typography of your book, such as line spacing and indentations. This will ensure that your book is easy to read and looks professional.

4. Create a professional cover: Create a cover that is visually appealing and that represents the genre and subject matter of your book. You can use pre-designed templates or hire a professional designer to create a custom cover.

5. Consider an ISBN: Consider getting an ISBN (International Standard Book Number) for your book. This will make it easier for bookstores and libraries to order and stock your book.

6. Format for e-book and print: Make sure to format your book for both e-book and print versions, as both formats have different requirements.

7. Test your formatting: Once you have finished

PUBLISHING AND DISTRIBUTION OPTIONS

Once you have written, edited, and designed your book, it's time to publish and distribute it. There are various options available for self-publishing authors, each with its own pros and cons. Here are a few popular options:

1. E-book publishing: E-books can be published and distributed through online retailers such as Amazon Kindle Direct Publishing, Barnes & Noble Nook Press, and Apple Books. This is a quick and easy way to get your book out to a global audience.

2. Print-on-demand: Print-on-demand (POD) services such as Amazon KDP Print, and IngramSpark allow you to print and

distribute physical copies of your book without having to worry about inventory or upfront costs.

3. Vanity publishing: Vanity publishing is a service that will publish and distribute your book in return for a fee. This option can be costly and may not offer the same level of control as other self-publishing options.

4. Traditional publishing: Traditional publishing is where you submit your manuscript to a publishing company, and they decide whether to publish it or not. You will get a royalty for each book sold and the publisher will take care of all the publishing and distribution process.

5. Hybrid publishing: Hybrid publishing is a combination of self-publishing and traditional publishing. The author pays for some or all of the costs of publishing, but the publisher provides services such as editing, design, and distribution.

It's important to research each option and to choose the one that best suits your book and your goals. By understanding the different publishing and distribution options available, you'll be able to make informed decisions about how to get your book to readers. For more info on how to properly execute all of the above make sure you check out **BookRichUniversity.com** or use our software at **BookRich.io**

CHAPTER III

MONETIZING
YOUR BOOK

Monetizing your book is the process of making money from your book. There are various ways to monetize your book, including:

1. Royalties: Royalties are payments made to the author for each book sold. This is the most common way to monetize a book.
2. Book sales: You can also make money by selling your book directly to readers, either through your own website or at events such as book signings.
3. Speaking engagements: If you're an expert in your field, you may be able to monetize your book by speaking at events and conferences.
4. Online courses: If you have a lot of knowledge about a specific subject, you can create an online course based on your book.
5. Coaching or consulting: If you have expertise in a specific area, you may be able to monetize your book by offering coaching or consulting services.

6. Affiliate marketing: You can monetize your book by using affiliate marketing, where you include links to products or services related to your book and earn a commission for each sale made through your links.
7. Product creation: You can create and sell other products related to your book, such as workbooks, study guides, or audio versions of the book.
8. Sponsorships and advertising: If you have a large following, you may be able to monetize your book by securing sponsorships or advertising deals.

It's important to remember that not all monetization strategies will work for every book or author. It's important to research different options and to choose the ones that best suit your book and your goals. Before we begin learning how to monetize your book you must learn two important concepts in the book publishing industry: Royalties and Rights.

Royalties refer to the payments made to an author for each copy of their book that is sold. The amount of the royalty varies depending on the publisher and the terms of the contract. Royalties can be based on a percentage of the retail price, a flat fee per book, or a combination of both. Typically, royalties range from 5-25% of the retail price for traditional publishing, and up to 70% for self-publishing.

Rights refer to the legal ownership of the content of a book. When an author signs a publishing contract, they typically grant certain rights to the publisher, such as the right to publish and distribute the book in certain formats and territories. The publisher will typically pay the author royalties for the use of these rights.

There are different types of rights that authors can grant to publishers, such as:

- World rights: the publisher has the right to publish the book in any language, anywhere in the world.
- North American rights: the publisher has the right to publish the book in North America.
- Electronic rights: the publisher has the right to publish the book in electronic formats such as e-books.
- Audio rights: the publisher has the right to create an audiobook version of the book.

It's important for authors to understand the rights they are granting to publishers and to negotiate terms that are favorable to them. This can include retaining certain rights, such as electronic rights, to be able to self-publish an e-book version of the book.

Below are 15 streams of Income that you can generate from your book with step-by-step instructions that you can use to implement them immediately.

1/15 – Getting Books in Hand (Physical Book)

Softcover books, also known as paperbacks, remain popular among readers due to their more affordable cost compared to hardcovers. Hardcovers, on the other hand, are considered more prestigious and carry a higher price tag. However, self-published authors and best-selling traditional authors can take advantage of bulk ordering discounts for hardcovers, which is why they often give away large numbers of hard-cover books at events. Digital versions of books, in the form of eBooks, are easily accessible through smartphones and offer convenient reading options while on-the-go. Additionally, eBook sellers typically offer higher royalties to authors, with a rate of 70% of the retail price. The deal gets sweeter when you realize that most eBook sellers now pay authors 70% of the retail price in royalties.

Once you decide what format you are going to publish (I believe AND is better than OR so I say do them all) You want to consider publishing under your own publishing company.

Starting your own company when self-publishing a book offers several advantages. One of the main advantages is that it allows you to separate your personal finances from your business finances. This means that your business income and expenses can be tracked and reported separately, making it easier to manage your finances and keep your personal assets separate from your business assets.

Another advantage is that it allows you to have more control over your business. When you self-publish a book as an individual, you may be limited in the types of business activities you can undertake. However, by starting your own company, you can set up different departments and hire employees to help you with different aspects of your business, such as marketing, sales, and distribution.

Additionally, starting your own company can also provide you with certain legal protections. For example, if someone were to sue you for something related to your book, your personal assets would be protected if your business is set up as a separate entity.

Lastly, starting your own company also gives you the opportunity to expand your business and create multiple streams of income. You can leverage the success of your book and turn it into a full-fledged business with multiple products and services.

Set up a Publishing Company

-   Research Your Options

There are generally three main options for business types:

- Sole Proprietorship
- LLC
- S-Corporation

A sole proprietorship is an unincorporated business that you run yourself. In the US, you claim this under your social security number for taxes. This is the easiest way to start.

An LLC is a limited liability company that is taxed similarly to a sole proprietorship. However, it is an incorporated business and separates and protects your personal assets from business assets under limited liability.

An S-Corporation is an incorporated business and gives more tax advantages and savings.

-   Decide on a Business Name

Now choose a name and ensure that it is not trademarked or already taken. This may seem obvious, but you want to choose a business name that is professional and fits your brand.

- Finalize the Business Type

Now that you have your business name chosen, you can **finalize the set-up** of your publishing company.

- Set Up Your Business Bank Account

Once you have your EIN, you can now apply for a business bank account. Each bank has a different process and requirements for setting up a business account. Therefore, consult with **your local bank** for more details.

- Register a Domain Name for Your Publishing Company
- Learn the Laws Related to Your Business

Make sure you **learn the laws** related to your business. For example, in the US, there are laws about collecting sales tax when you sell books at live events and it differs from state to state. You may also need to register for a sales tax license in your state and/or your city.

Purchase Your ISBN Numbers

ISBNs are free in many countries, provided either by the government or a publicly administered branch. However, in the US ISBN numbers are administered by <u>Bowker</u> and <u>Nielsen</u> respectively and require you to pay.

To get an ISBN you would go to <u>myidentifiers.com</u>, run by Bowker, the only company that is authorized to administer the ISBN program in the United States. You can purchase ISBNs as a single unit or in bulk of 10, 100 or 1000.

As soon as you purchase your ISBN through Bowker or the International equivalent in your local area, and you publish your book, you should register for an account at <u>Bowkerlink</u>. This is an automated tool that will add your book to Bowker's <u>Books In Print</u> and Global Books In Print.

Keep in mind that you can only use an ISBN once. The ISBN is a unique number for that particular book, and can be assigned once, and only once, to that title. It can't be used with any other book in the future, even second versions of the same book.

You don't need an ISBN to sell in each individual country. ISBNs are international, they are just assigned locally. A US-based publisher can purchase their ISBN through Bowker but can stock their book worldwide using that ISBN.

You need an ISBN for every specific format of the book and any new versions. Want to sell your book in print, as an eBook, and also as an audiobook? That's great, however, you need a different ISBN for each one. If you want to publish a revised and updated version, you'll also need a new ISBN. (This doesn't cover fixing some typos and errors).

If you create a series of books, you can't use the same ISBN for them. You can use the same ISSN, however. Many fiction and non-fiction authors have an ISSN number assigned to their book series. ISSN stands for <u>International Standard Series Number</u> and can be purchased from the <u>Library of Congress</u>. However, each book in the series will need its own ISBN.

Most Self-publishing platforms will provide you an ISBN number for free or a low cost but keep in mind that if you choose that option your book will be registered to their platform instead of your own entity ie: My publishing company is 1Brick Publishing so If I buy my own ISBN number my books will display "Published by 1Brick Publishing." If I decide to use Amazon's Kindle Direct Publishing ISBN number by book will display "Self-Published or Independently Published" which will negatively affect your ability to get publicity.

Assign an ISBN number to Your Title

Log into your Bowker's account by visiting https://www.myidentifiers.com/

Once you sign in, hit the My Account dropdown tab and choose "Manage ISBNs"

This will show you the ISBN numbers that are available to you and to the right of that number you will choose "Assign title"

Follow the directions necessary to assign your title. Once completed jot down this number below as you will need it for your Copyright/Disclaimer page as well as for uploading your book to Amazon and Ingram Sparks

Title of Book: _____

Format: _____

ISBN#_____

Research/determine price point for all formats

Keep your book price low and affordable. Any ebook priced above $4.99 is too much for a self-published author in my opinion (Unless you are a celebrity or well-known public figure)

Your paperback or hard cover should be priced between $9.99 and $14.99. I know many new authors who price their paperback or hard cover between $15 and $30; This is a mistake. Yes, you will make some money from friends and family who want to support you but if you really want to sell a lot of books you have to appeal to people who don't know you. The book market shows that book buyers just don't pay that much for an author they don't know.

I know you want to get compensated for the time it took you to write the book but think of the long game not just the short-term gain. Even if you sell it at between $9.99 and $14.99, you still make a good margin since your printing cost will only be between $2 and $5.

Hardcover Price: $_____
Paperback Price: $_____
Ebook Price: $_____
*Audiobook Price: $_____

*If you are going to use ACX.com to publish your audiobook on Audible and iTunes then you will not be able to set your price yourself. If you use a different platform you will be able to.

Research/determine sales categories

Amazon has over 16,000+ and there isn't one spot where you can view them all (Not that you would want to). They key to finding the right sales category is to find similar books that already exist and view the categories that they are using.

For example, below is the categories for my book Hu$$lenomics

Product details

Paperback: 186 pages
Publisher: 1Brick Publishing (August 15, 2019)
Language: English
ISBN-10: 1949303047
ISBN-13: 978-1949303049
Product Dimensions: 5.5 x 0.4 x 8.5 inches
Shipping Weight: 9.6 ounces (View shipping rates and policies)
Average Customer Review: ⭐⭐⭐☆☆ ⌄ 8 customer reviews
Amazon Best Sellers Rank: #12,956 in Books (See Top 100 in Books)
     #183 in Entrepreneurship (Books)
     #5 in Music Business (Books)
     #20 in Rap Music (Books)

Below name three books that are similar to yours and their categories:

Name of Book   Book Category

1._____

2._____

3._____

Research/determine keywords/tags

Finding the right keywords for your book will not only help your book become discoverable by those who are looking for it but also help you sell books by putting you in the ranks with other popular books in that category.

<u>Best practices</u>

- Combine keywords in the most logical order. Customers search for "military science fiction" but probably not for "fiction science military"
- Use up to seven keywords or short phrases. Keep an eye on the character limit in the text field
- Before publishing, search for your book's title and keywords on Amazon. If you get irrelevant or unsatisfying results, make some changes. When searching, look at the suggestions that appear in the "Search" field drop down
- Think like a reader. Imagine how you'd search if you were a customer

<u>Keywords to avoid</u>

- Information covered elsewhere in your book's metadata (title, contributors, etc.)
- Subjective claims about quality (e.g. "best novel ever")
- Time-sensitive statements ("new," "on sale," "available now")
- Information common to most items in the category ("book")
- Spelling errors

- Variants of spacing, punctuation, capitalization, and pluralization ("80GB" and "80 GB," "computer" and "computers", etc.). Exception: Words translated in more than one way (e.g. "Mao Zedong" or "Mao Tse-tung," "Hanukkah" or "Chanukah"
- Anything misrepresentative like the name of an author not associated with your book. This kind of information can create a confusing customer experience.
- Quotation marks in search terms. Single words work better than phrases, and specific words work better than general ones. If you enter "complex suspenseful whodunit," only people who type all of those words will find your book. For better results, enter this: complex suspenseful whodunit. Customers can search for any of those words and find your book
- Amazon program names like as "Kindle Unlimited" or "KDP Select"

Jot Down a few keywords below:

_____

_____

_____

_____

_____

_____

_____

_____

_____

_____

_____

Setup a Kindle Direct Publishing Account

Upload print book files to KDP.Amazon.com (Formerly CreateSpace). It's very user friendly so I won't spell out the directions here. Just make sure you DO NOT choose the "Expanded Distribution" option as it will limit your sales

Setup an Ingram Sparks Account

ACCOUNT SETUP

If you have not yet registered for an IngramSpark account, please follow the steps below. If you already have an account but would like to read about the Account Setup Tasks.

Log on to http://www.ingramspark.com/ and click on "CREATE ACCOUNT."

This takes you to our Create Your Account page. You will be asked basic but pertinent information to create your account. Once you have completed the information, please click on the blue "Continue" button to move forward.

You will receive a message similar to the one below:

Thank you, xxxxx for creating an IngramSpark account.

To complete the setup process just click on the link in the email that they just sent to you. You have 7 days to activate your account, or you can easily start over by returning to the homepage at www.ingramspark.com.

Open your email to access the account verification link, and then log in to your IngramSpark account using your email address and password used on the Create Your Account page.

After logging in and agreeing to general terms of the site, you will be taken through four agreements. You will be required to accept the Global POD agreement and the Global Ebook agreement, but it does not mean you are required to use those services. It simply means that you have those services on our account if you choose to use them later.

- Global POD - Print-on-Demand (POD) services via our Lightning Source companies in the US, UK, AU, as well as the Global Connect and Espresso POD networks.
- Global Ebook - Ebook distribution services to all of their Ebook Distribution Partners except Amazon Kindle and Apple.

- Amazon (Kindle) Ebook (optional) - If you want to distribute your Ebooks to Amazon Kindle. (You can opt out if you are uploading directly to Kindle).
- Apple (Agency) Ebook (optional) - If you want to distribute your Ebooks to Apple's US and International iBooks and iTunes stores.

Once you select "I Accept" for the agreements, you will enter your electronic signature and title (e.g., owner). Click on the blue "Sign Agreements" button, and you are ready to access your IngramSpark account!

Upload Your Book Files to KDP

Login to kdp.Amazon.com and upload your book files. You will need your Book Cover PDF, The PDF of your book interior, Your ISBN#, Epub/Mobi files, etc; Follow the directions, they are pretty straight forward. When you get to pricing DO NOT choose "Expanded Distrubution"

Upload Your Book Files to Ingram Sparks

Login to IngramSparks.com and upload your book files. You will need the same as above... Your Book Cover PDF, The PDF of your book interior, Your ISBN#, Epub/Mobi files, etc; Follow the directions, they are pretty straight forward.

Review digital page proofs at KDP

Once you upload all of your files, Amazon will put it through a quality review, and you should receive a digital proof within

24-48 hours. This digital proof once approved can make your book live on Amazon, but I would suggest waiting until you get your physical proof before approving for sale.

Order print (POD) copy from KDP

After you verify the digital proof, place an order through KDP for a print copy of your book. This usually takes a few days for you to receive, and it will give you one last chance to review your book for any obvious errors.

Review digital page proofs at Ingram Sparks

Once you upload all of your files, IngramSparks will put it through a quality review, and you should be ready to view your digital proof almost immediately. This digital proof once approved can make your book live and available for sale at all independent bookstores and retailers, but I would suggest waiting until you get your physical proof before approving for sale.

Order print (POD) copy from Ingram Sparks

After you verify the digital proof, place an order through IngramSparks for a print copy of your book. This usually takes a few days, depending on what shipping option you chose, and it again gives you one last chance to review your book for any obvious errors.

***Once you receive both physical proofs from Amazon and Ingram-Sparks decide which service you want to use to buy your own copies at cost. I prefer IngramSparks because they ship faster than Amazon but sometimes if I'm not in a rush I choose Amazon because their quality is slightly better.

Setup Your Book on Google Play

Many people are focused on the Apple ecosystem and forget about the potential reach of Google's platforms. One such platform is Google Play Books, an online bookstore integrated within the Google Play store. With 2.5 billion Android users, this is a significant opportunity for authors to reach a global audience. Previously, getting your book on Google Play Books required an approval period and possibly a waiting list. However, in 2020, Google made it easier for independent authors to open a publisher account without the need for an approval period.

HERE'S HOW TO PUBLISH YOUR BOOK ON GOOGLE PLAY IN 7 EASY STEPS

Step 1: Create your Google Play Partner account

To publish your book on Google Play, you can visit the author landing page at g.co/play/publish, and click on the "Get Started" button to create your account. You will need to have a Google account to proceed, but if you have a Gmail account, you are all set. If not, you will need to create a Google account.

Step 2: Enter your financial information

To receive royalties from Google Play, you need to provide your payment and tax information, and link your bank account. Keep in mind that it can take up to 12 days for Google to review and activate your account. To avoid delays with your book launch, it is recommended to set up your book on the platform at least two weeks prior to your planned release date, especially if it is your first time publishing a book.

Step 3: Create your first book

After setting up your account, you can access the dashboard and click on "Add your first book." At this point, you will need to decide whether you want to make your eBook available for sale on Google Play or simply provide a preview of it on Google Books.

It's important to understand the difference between Google Play and Google Books, as they are two distinct platforms. Google Play is an online store where you can sell your e-book, while Google Books is an online index of full-text books that have been digitized by Google to make them searchable on search engines. When you publish on Google Play, your book will automatically be indexed on Google Books. However, if you want to only offer a preview on Google Books and not sell it on Google Play, you can select that option. This can be useful for authors who are enrolled in KDP Select and want their book to be indexed in the Google Books library. Keep in mind that you should have already purchased your own ISBN number and not choose the option to "Get a Google Book ID" even though it's free.

Step 4: Fill in your books' metadata

The metadata process on Google Play Books is divided into four steps:

- About the book
- Genres
- Contributors
- Settings

About the book

When publishing your book on the Google Play store, it is important to optimize your title, subtitle, and book description for the platform. To do this, you can copy and paste the blurb you have already created for your book. If you want to publish your book immediately, leave the "On-sale date" field blank. If you are publishing a pre-order, make sure to fill in the launch date. On the "About the book" page, you can also take advantage of the option to "add a related book" at the bottom. This is a great opportunity to connect your book with other books, even if they are not in the same series, such as an anthology, a box set or another series in the same universe. One last thing on the "About the book" page: Google gives you the opportunity to "add a related book" at the bottom. This is a great chance to link your book with other ones, even if they're not in the series (i.e. an anthology, a box set, or another series in the same universe).

Genres

Google Play has a unique approach when it comes to categorizing books. Unlike other stores, it doesn't limit the number of genres you can select. Additionally, it allows you to pick categories from the BISAC (North America) or BIC (UK and Australia) systems. To maximize your book's visibility, it is important to carefully choose all the categories that are relevant to your book. This will take some time, but it will be worth it since categories play a crucial role in Google's search algorithms.

Contributors

The next step is simple; you will need to provide your author name and author bio. Additionally, you can also mention any other contributors involved in the creation of your book, such as editors, illustrators, translators, or ghostwriters.

Preview settings

Google Play offers more flexibility compared to other platforms by allowing you to choose the amount of the book that readers will be able to preview using the "Look Inside" feature. Keep in mind that the minimum preview allowed is 20%.

Another feature that you can control is the amount of text that readers can copy-paste from your book. You can set it to 0% or any other percentage you prefer. Additionally, Google Play also gives you the option to opt in or out of DRM encryption.

If one of your objectives is to improve your book's visibility on Google Books search, make sure to click on "Show advanced settings" and fill in those fields. These fields can help optimize your book's presence on the index we discussed in step 3.

Step 5: Upload your book and cover files

This step is straightforward, you will simply need to have your files ready. Specifically, you will need the following files:

- Your front cover image
- Your EPUB or PDF
- Your back cover image (optional)

One of the great features of Google Play is that once your files have been processed and accepted, you can add "Content Reviewers" by entering their email addresses. This allows you to give early access to your book for free, making it a useful tool for sharing advance copies with beta readers or reviewers.

It's worth noting that you can add Content Reviewers even after you've finished setting up your book on Google Play. There are some requirements for Content Reviewers, such as having a Google account, but most people should meet them. This feature allows you to continue to share your book with readers even after the book is published.

Step 6: Set your book's price

Google Play Books offers the ability to set different prices for different regions and currencies. To ensure that your book is competitively priced in each currency, it is advisable to take advantage of this feature. This way you can make sure that your book is affordable for readers in different regions, and you can also earn more revenue.

For instance, you can set your book's price at £0.99 in the UK and Ireland, €0.99 in the Eurozone, and $0.99 in other regions. This way, the book will be affordably priced in different currencies, and you can attract more readers.

It's worth noting that the "additional settings" allow you to make these prices temporary. This can be useful if you want to offer promotional pricing at launch. This way, you can attract more readers and generate more sales by offering a discounted price for a limited time.

Step 7: Review and publish

The only thing left to do is to make sure you've entered everything correctly, and George Bush the Button aka hit the "Publish" button.

Now would be a good time to return to step 5. Your files should have been processed by now, and you can add in your "Content Reviewers" just before you publish. This will allow you to share your book with beta readers or reviewers in advance and get their feedback before making it available to the general public.

2/15 – Gifting Your Story w/ Sound (Audiobook)

If you don't have an audio version of your book, then you are leaving money on the table. I sell a good portion of books via Audible and iTunes because many of my fans drive Uber, Lyft, and or Trucks, so they have limited time to read.

Recording your own audiobook can be a great way to connect with your audience and promote your book through speaking engagements. It allows potential clients to hear your speaking style and can make it easier for them to envision you as a speaker at their event. Additionally, it can be cost-effective as you won't need to pay for a narrator. However, it's important to keep in mind that recording your own audiobook can be time-consuming and may require additional equipment or software. It's also important to consider whether you have the skills and experience necessary to produce a high-quality recording. If you decide to outsource, you can find professional narrators on platforms like ACX or Upwork. It's essential to research and select a narrator that matches your desired style and tone.

Recording your audiobook using a MV-88 microphone and your iPhone is a cost-effective and simple way to produce a high-quality recording. The MV-88 is a portable microphone that is designed to work with iOS devices and can be attached directly to your iPhone. This setup allows you to record your audiobook in a variety of settings and can produce a professional-sounding recording.

Sending the files to someone at Fiverr.com to clean them up is a great way to ensure that the final recording is of the highest quality. The audio editor will be able to remove any background noise or unwanted sounds, equalize the levels, and apply any other necessary audio processing.

Once the files are cleaned up, you can then upload them to ACX.com, which is a platform that connects authors with audiobook narrators and audio producers. This platform will allow you to distribute your audiobook to a wide range of retailers, such as Audible, Amazon, and Apple Books. By using this platform, you will be able to reach a larger audience and increase your potential revenue.

That's correct, ACX provides detailed information on the file format and technical specifications for audiobook recordings, including bit rate, sample rate, and file type. Recording in a professional studio environment with an experienced audio engineer can help ensure that your files meet these specifications and produce a high-quality recording. Studio recording also provides an opportunity to record in a controlled environment that reduces background noise and other unwanted sounds.

The audio engineer can also help you with editing your files to meet the ACX specifications and to ensure that the final recording is of the highest quality. They can help you with things like removing background noise, equalizing the levels, and applying other necessary audio processing. Additionally, booking studio time to record your book can give you the opportunity to work with professional equipment and have the added benefit of a trained engineer to guide you through the recording process.

If you decided to outsource your audiobook, ACX allows you to audition their Voiceover actors but your book must be available for sale through Amazon so you can assign yourself as the author.

Fiverr.com and Upwork also offers voiceover actors

Self-Publishing Audiobooks: Publishing Options for Your Audiobook

Once you've wrapped recording and editing, next up is making it accessible for download. In order to do that you'll need to choose a publishing platform and determine the price of your audiobook. Since I mentioned ACX previously we will start there but keep in mind this isn't the only option you have even though most believe this to be true.

ACX

Currently, the most popular digital platform for producing and distributing audio books is Amazon's ACX which stands for Audiobook Creation Exchange. ACX uses Audible as its distributor to Amazon and iTunes, the two biggest retailers of audiobooks.

In working with ACX, you must make two decisions,

First, you must decide whether you are going to record your audio yourself or hire a voiceover actor to do it. As previously stated I strongly suggest you use your own voice but if you do decide to use a VO actor you must decide if you will (1) pay the VO actor an upfront fee for the work (typically between $100 and $1000 per finished hour) but no royalty paid to the VO actor for any sales, or (2) to split your share of the audiobook royalties 50/50 with the VO actor and pay no upfront fee.

The second decision is whether to sell the audiobook through Audible on an exclusive or non-exclusive basis.

If you grant exclusive rights to ACX, then you will receive 40% of the retail sales. However, you must agree not to distribute the audiobook through any other channels or in any other audio format, including your own website. An exclusive agreement with ACX does not affect your right to sell other versions of your book, just audio.

If you choose the non-exclusive option, then the royalty rate is 25%. In this instance, you don't have the option to split royalties with the VO actor and must pay them a flat fee.

How does pricing work with ACX?

When it comes to pricing, keep in mind that ACX has full control. You'll have strict distribution agreements, and you won't have direct access to your audience.

- ACX sets the price for you based on length, as follows:
  - Under 1 hour: under $7
  - 1 – 3 hours: $7 – $10
  - 3 – 5 hours: $10 – $20
  - 5 – 10 hours: $15 – $25
  - 10 – 20 hours: $20 – $30
  - Over 20 hours: $25 – 35

Distribution agreements: If you exclusively publish with ACX, you retain 40% of the sales. If you're publishing elsewhere as well, you're only paid 25% of the sales.

Access to your audience: Even if you were to get amplified by the Audible algorithm, you aren't provided with access to your customer base.

This means It's hard for independent authors to build an email list to leverage for future sales. To circumvent this it would be a good idea to do add a call to action in the book itself to sign up for an email list. ACX is a great option because Amazon offers the potential opportunity to be discovered by a new audience—after all, it's Amazon, the biggest mall on the planet.

To get started go to ACX.com using your Amazon account login and follow the direction to establish an account.

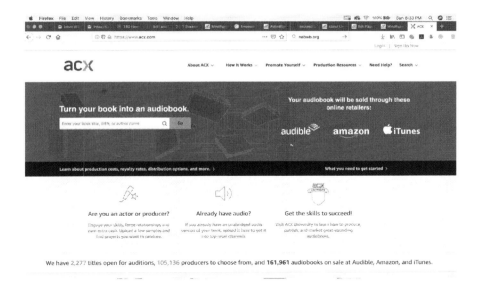

Findaway Voices

Findaway Voices is another popular platform for production and distribution of Audiobooks. In fact, If I were you, I would keep a close eye on this platform as it was recently acquired by Spotify which is looking to dominate the audiobook space and everything sound. Findaway offer packages to support audiobook authors from draft to publish, including narration, editing, marketing, distribution and sales.

Different from ACX, Findaway provides authors with access and distribution to more than 40 audiobook retailers and library platforms, including Audible, Apple, Google, Nook and many more. Essentially, Findaway Voices acts as a pipeline between you and multiple distribution platforms.

How does pricing work with Findaway Voices?

You'll have more control over the price of your audiobook depending on which distribution channels you choose.

For example, if you work with Findaway Voices to distribute your books on Amazon, you'll still be locked into the pricing structure I mentioned earlier. With other retailers though, you'll be able to set your list price.

- Pricing. Authors keep 80% of the royalties and pay a distribution fee of 20% of the royalties you earn.
- Distribution Agreements. They do not lock authors into exclusive contracts, and they assist authors with removing audiobooks from ACX exclusivity.

Findaway Voices is a good choice for established audiobook authors that are looking to get away from ACX exclusivity and we are yet to see what ways Spotify will enhance this platform but I can only imagine it will help authors sell more copies and get more visibility.

Visit www.FinawayVoices.com to Register for your FREE account

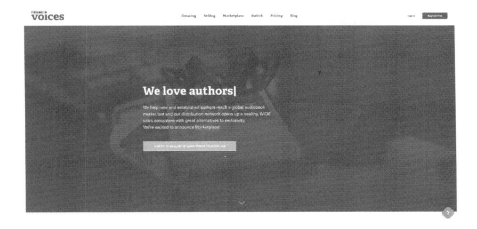

Kobo Writing Life

Since Sept. 2019, authors have the ability to upload their audiobooks directly through Kobo Writing Life and sell them on Kobo.

Their audiobooks will be published in a few simple steps:

- Describe audiobook
- Upload cover image, audio files
- Create a custom Table of Contents
- Enter pricing and hit publish
- Audiobook will be published within 72 hours

No exclusivity is required. KWL usually encourages authors to publish and distribute with multiple platforms to broaden their audience.

Visit: https://www.kobo.com/ca/en/p/writinglife to open an account

Soundwise

Soundwise is the new solution for authors who want to sell audiobooks directly to listeners and build their own audience, without paying the high fees of the traditional platforms.

Soundwise differs from ACX in many key ways:

- You're not up against an algorithm, or other authors. Soundwise is not a marketplace. Audiobook authors use Soundwise to host their audiobooks securely and deliver the audio to listeners' mobile devices. Listeners buy audiobooks directly from the author.
- You can build an email list you own. Listeners are buying directly from you, and you own your email list. This is critical for any audiobook author's long-term career—having an email list allows you to stay in touch with and sell directly to former customers as you produce more books and audiobooks.

An expanding reader/listener email list is arguably the most important asset of any indie author.

- You can fully track and measure your marketing strategies. You'll be able to optimize your marketing strategy and sales funnels, which will also be critical for future audiobook sales.

- The platform is easy to use. You could be ready for sales within the hour. Audio hosting, payment, promo codes, analytics, mobile and web content delivery are all in one place.

- You can build a community, through direct contact with your audience. Listeners can leave comments and you have the option to reply.

- It's secure. Though listeners can listen offline, they won't be able to move or copy your files.

How does pricing work with Soundwise?

You have full control over your pricing with Soundwise and have the potential to keep 100% of your profits, while Audible will take 60% to 80% of your sales.

- Pricing. With Soundwise's starter plan ($10 a month if you sign up annually), you retain 90% of each transaction. You keep 100% of your audiobook sales under the Plus, Pro and Platinum plans.

  This means, profit wise, five Soundwise sales are equal to 25 Audible sales. This means in most cases, the ROI of your marketing spend will always be higher (unless you're lucky enough to really be favored by Audible's algorithm).

Flexibility. With full control over your pricing structure, you can be more flexible and test strategies like price promotions, bundles sales, limited time discounts, exchanging audiobooks for listener reviews, and more.

- Distribution agreements. There are none, you're fully in control.

Visit: https://mysoundwise.com/ to get started

3/15 - Getting Straight to the Point (Ebooks)

Ebooks are a how to's without the stories or fluff. You can break down your book into individual files that can be sold separately and for a higher price. Ebooks are different from the digital version of your book because eBooks cut straight to the chase and give readers a step-by-step guide on doing something without the supporting stories.

Step 1: Create a Killer Title that Sells

The master key to selling massive copies of your eBook is the title! All titles for eBooks should be very clear as to what someone will be getting when they read your book. Your title should also be long and descriptive. For instance, the reason why my eBook on how to write eBook's is called "8 Steps to Writing and Publishing Your eBook in Less Than 4 Hours + How to Sell Your First 100 Copies," is because whoever buys the eBook will know exactly what they're getting from the book. They know that after they finish reading the book, they will get eight steps that's going to teach them how to write and publish an eBook, they're going to do it in four hours or less, and I'm going to teach them how to sell their 100 copies. Now it's your turn. Pull all of your How to's from your book and below write your killer title for each one and be as descriptive as possible:

_____

_____

_____

_____

_____

_____

_____

_____

_____

_____

_____

_____

_____

_____

_____

_____

_____

_____

_____

Step 2: Create a Great eBook Cover

This is one of the few times where I am going to say it is OK to judge a book by its cover. Your book cover has a DIRECT IMPACT to your sales so make sure your cover is good and eye-catching. Here are your options below to get your eBook designed:

Option 1: Canva.com - Canva provides a lot of great FREE book cover templates (901) and free stock photos that you can use to make a very eye appealing eBook cover.

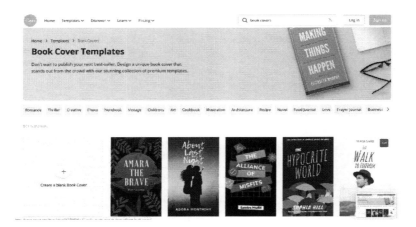

Option 2: Hire someone on fiverr.com - Fiverr is a marketplace for entrepreneurs to connect with other entrepreneurs who are looking to sell their products and/or services. I use someone that charges me $10. You could simply just type in eBook cover, and you will see different samples of eBook covers.

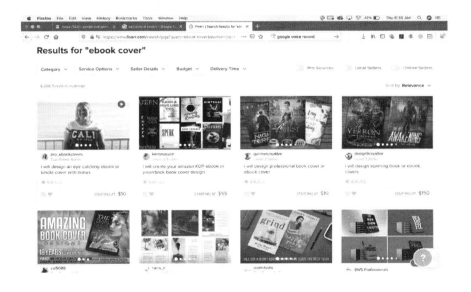

Option 3: MyeCoverMaker.com - There's a software called myecovermaker and you can now create your own ebook covers very quickly. I would only suggest this option if you have intentions of creating a lot of eBook covers (Or you can create a side hustle and provide the service to the world). The great thing about myecovermaker, is that they have a software that allows you to create 3d versions of your eBook for marketing purposes.

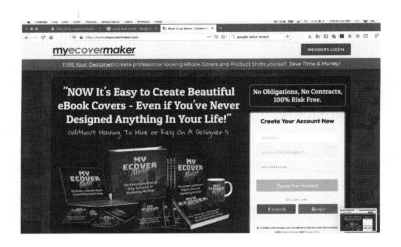

The one thing about a great eBook cover is that you always want the colors to be vibrant and you want the cover to pop. You want it to be eye catching you want it to be something that when people see they immediately are going to run towards it. So keep that in mind when you're putting your cut your eBook cover together. Here are some examples of some great covers:

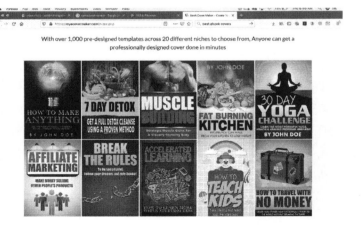

Step 3: Edit Then Design Your eBook's Interior

This will mostly be the step that takes the most time (2hours) but it's worth it since once you do it right you can eat (make money) off of this eBook FOREVER! Identify the word processing software you're going to use most likely it will be Microsoft Word or whatever word processing document software you're comfortable with. Most of those word processing software's have nice design templates that you can use so I want you to find a design that you like and literally, edit your book, and start to design the interiors.

This first edit is simply to make sure the book reads and flows the way you want it to. You can choose to be super critical, or you can just ask yourself, "Does this get my point across?" I'm not saying but out a mediocre product but don't let the fear of being attacked by librarians force you to spend a lot of time on this step. As long as you think it's effective to your target audience then you're good.

The second edit is for Grammar and punctuation, and this MUST be done. At this point, you have two options: You can edit for grammar and punctuation yourself with a software (I personally use Grammarly) or go to Fiverr or to Upwork.com and find somebody to edit it for you. Option two will take more time.

Once you get the edited copy back, you put it back into your word processor, use the template that they created, and I want you to save it as a PDF. So, if you use a Microsoft Word or any other word type publishing software, you're going to hit File, Save as PDF. Once you hit file save as PDF, I want you to now open that PDF as a preview then drag and drop your cover as the first page into that PDF. This is going to be the document that you're going to sell. Anytime somebody purchases your book you will deliver this main document.

Step 4: Choose a Place to Sell Your eBook

Now it's time to set up your bookstore or the platform where someone can purchase your book. There are many options: You have Shopify or Clickfunnels, you can do a WordPress website using an app called Woo-Commerce, you can use Samcart or you can use PayPal. PayPal allows you to create products and services and provide links to those products and services or you can use our BookRich® app which is all in one.

Please do your research on each of these options and choose the best options that work for you. Once you find the place that you're going to sell it. You also need to figure out how much you're going to sell it for. Depending on your marketing you can start at $1 and you can go up to whatever you think is an appropriate price. I like to keep my eBooks between $1 and $97 to make it affordable.

4/15 – Turn Your Book into an Academy (Self-Study Online Program)

Many readers want to experience your content on a deeper level. As a result, I've created online coaching programs for most of my books, including my memoir, From the Block to the Bank. Clients can access the content 24/7. The best thing about this approach is that you only need to create this once, and then you can increase your influence, impact, and income for the rest of your life! I call this Mailbox Money!

As of now you've written the book that solves the problem, and some people may be able to implement your solutions just by reading the book, but majority of people will need more assistance. While your advice may be the best answer to their problems, not everyone can afford to pay for one-on-one coaching. Sometimes their schedules are so crazy they don't even have 15 minutes to spare for a coaching call.

These people are best served by your courses, which can be less expensive than one-on-one coaching and can fit into their schedule as time allows. These passive income streams can sell for years and years almost on auto-pilot, but you need to create relevant content and have a killer name that will stand out from the rest of the competition.

In this section you'll re-examine your target market and their needs as well as open up your creative mind to start brainstorming ideas for a course. Don't overthink your answers and don't edit yourself during the brainstorming phase. Put yourself in your target market's shoes and dream big.

Let's get started...

Step One: Find the topic that makes your WHOLE tribe excited times 10x! It's a fine line choosing a topic that you love talking about versus a topic that your audience wants. However, it's vitally important if you want a solid return on your investment. Ask yourself are you going to create a course based on your whole book or just a few topics from your book.

You may love talking about X, but if your audience is far more interested in Y, then that's where your course should focus. If you want to make a profit, focus on what your people will pay to learn! Remember, even if a topic sounds easy to YOU, it's not easy for others to learn and they will happily pay you to teach them. How do you discover these hot topics? Pay attention to what your audience is saying.

Look at your most popular social media posts, top performing social media articles or blogs, and most common search terms. Look at the comments on your social media post and or blog if you have one, too. Do you have a group or participate in groups where your ideal clients hang out? Pay attention there as well. Another person's vent about what's missing in their life or what they wish they could find is another person's opportunity to create something valuable.

If you're still struggling, create a poll that includes the top 5 topics you believe are follower favorites. Publicize the poll on social media and email it to your list. Ask direct questions about what they want to learn and why.

In the end, successful sales come down to having a product that will yield the results your ideal clients want and need in their lives. So create a product that is client-focused and your sales will then become an awesome by-product, leading the way to creating more products to fill your library.

Exercise: Find out what your followers love.

What I THINK my fans want	What my fans ACTUALLY want
1.	1.
2.	2.
3.	3.
4.	4.
5.	5.
Most Popular Blog Post Topics	**Most Popular Social Media Topics**
1.	1.
2.	2.
3.	3.
4.	4.
5.	5.

Email List Responses	What's being said in my groups?
1.	1.
2.	2.
3.	3.
4.	4.
5.	5.

Survey Questions	Survey Responses
1.	1.
2.	2.
3.	3.
4.	4.
5.	5.

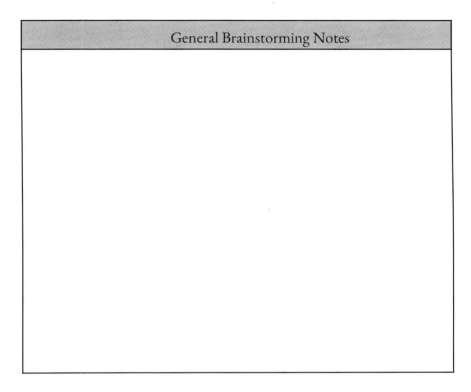

General Brainstorming Notes

STEP TWO: HOME IN ON YOUR SUBJECT WITH LASER-LIKE PRECISION

Some topics are better suited to courses than others. Even if your followers love it when you talk about your pedicures or haircuts, you can't quite build lessons around that! No matter how big or small a course you want to create, there needs to be actionable content so your students can achieve a certain result. You provide the roadmap while they provide the action.

You can provide explicit action steps (i.e. write 200 words a day) or more vague action steps based on their own research (i.e. subscribe to your favorite autoresponder platform). Based on your research in Step One, compare two of the frontrunner topics. Which one would make a more compelling course? Do you have enough information to create actionable content?

How much information do you have: Enough for a single webinar or enough for 10 lessons? While you're plotting out how much information you have on each topic, remember to keep your list focused and on topic. Sure, there will be dozens of subtopics but does each of them have a place in your course? Or will that just confuse your students? Also think about if these topics are analytical or emotional.

Analytical topics have facts to support them, so they are easier to work into a course whereas emotional topics are often more opinion-based and make for better blog posts.

It's time for some analyzing. Sometimes it's easiest to see what you have to work with when it's written out in list form. This can also be done using mind-mapping software, if that's your preference.

Exercise: Create a pros/cons list for your top two topics.

Front Runner Topic #1	
PROS	CONS

Front Runner Topic #1	
Is this an analytical or emotional topic?	

List the lessons you'll include in this course	
What actionable content will you include in this course?	

Brainstorming Notes

Front Runner Idea #2	
PROS	CONS

Is this an analytical or emotional topic?	
List the lessons you'll include in this course	
What actionable content will you include in this course?	

STEP THREE: SCOPE OUT THE COMPETITION (AND PLAN TO DO IT BETTER!)

In the business world, competition is a good thing. By looking at the competition prior to creating and launching your product, you'll know if your market has money to spend and if they're willing to spend it. Think of it as your competitors giving you some free market analysis!

Of course, if you're planning a course on "How to start an ecommerce store" and there are 900 other similar courses, you can still do it … but make sure yours is unique in some way. Regurgitating the same tips that can be found via google search won't motivate too many people to take your course seriously; or worse yet, they'll ask for refunds if they aren't learning anything new.

You are unique and no one else is quite like you, so make your course equally as unique. add your personality; add your voice; share lessons you've learned or case studies backing up why your methods work…and work better than your competitors' methods. Also brainstorm ways you can fill in the missing gaps your competitors may have left out. Maybe instead of recreating the wheel, you just create a course filling those gaps that your market is asking for.

One way to discover these gaps is to do a google search for that product and read the online reviews.

People are very quick to leave negative feedback so balance the negative reviews with the positive ones.

You may discover a real golden nugget in these reviews that will help fill a gap or make your course more unique.

Lastly, remember to create a stellar customer service experience for your customer. While this may not be related directly to creating your product, customer service is often the first and last impression your customer has of your company. Making it easy for them to ask questions, make a purchase, or even requesting a refund will make an indelible impression about your company and your attitude about customer care.

Creating a bestselling course is a mix of research, creativity, and market research. Follow all those steps and you'll be on your way to creating a superstar course.

Exercise: Compare competitive courses and analyze how yours can be different.

	Competitor #1	Competitor #2	Competitor #2
Name + Product Features			
Their target market (best guess based on their sales letter)			

What features are missing from their course?			
What promises are they making?			
What bonuses are they giving?			
What do their reviews say?			
Brainstorming Notes			
How is my product different from my other offerings?			

What can I add to my product?	
How can my product be (more) unique?	
How can I offer a different perspective on the same topic?	
What format do I want to use to create my course? (i.e. written, video, audio, a mix)	

How is my product aligned to my customers' buying behaviors?	
How will my product align with my mission statement?	
How will my product align to my company values?	

Is this idea trendy? Am I jumping in at the right time?	

General Notes

What is my customer service process? What can be improved?	

Exercise: Explore the gaps and subtopics of your main topic.

My Main Topic

Subtopics

Gaps in the Market

- What ideas are trending in my market today?

- What's missing from the market?

- What are my fans asking for?

- What are my current customers giving feed-back about?

- Can I tackle these gaps myself? Do I know some-one who can help me?

- Are people searching online for this?

STEP FOUR: NOW START THINKING OF KILLER NAMES FOR YOUR BESTSELLING COURSE!

Now that you have your course mapped out and have done some market research, it's time to start brainstorming some names. This process is always easier once you have a firm grip on what type of content you'll cover in your course; working backwards – fitting the content into a course name – is severely limiting. Make the course the best it can be, then think of a killer name afterward.

First, think about who your target market is for this course. You've done this already when writing your book so you are a step ahead! Take that client avatar and be sure this is who your course will serve. If not, make some revisions. Knowing who will purchase your course allows you to fine tune your marketing message and also be sure you're providing everything that ideal client needs to succeed.

A client avatar is a made-up compilation of all the features and demographics of your ideal client. These are made up "people," not necessarily people you already know.

Compare this process to the way fiction authors create the characters in their stories:

Authors have their general storyline in mind, they do their research, then they create the leading and supporting cast of characters.

Gather your data (remember the info from Step One) and give your client avatar a name.

You'll discover it's much easier to create your marketing messages, emails, and social media posts when you know exactly who you're speaking to and why they need your product.

Exercise: Think about your target audience and create a client avatar.

Target Market Demographics	Target Market Pain Points
Include age, gender, education level, hobbies, fears, passions, where they live, marital status, family life, beliefs...	What do they struggle with/are afraid of? What solution(s) are they willing to buy?

Create Client Avatar Profile	Give Client Avatar a Name

EXERCISE: Brainstorm course names using this core value template.

WHO does your course help?	
WHAT result are you promising?	
HOW will they benefit from your course?	

My course helps [target audience] learn how to [result] so they can [benefit].

My course helps _____ learn how to _____ so they can _____.

Killer Name Ideas

Exercise: Use this checklist to fine tune your name ideas.

Does your name idea:

- ❑ Represent the level of your students and their skillset?
- ❑ Accurately represent your industry?
- ❑ Explain the learning objective or benefits of your course?
- ❑ Sound complicated or is it easy-to-read?
- ❑ Use slang or is it grammatically, correct?
- ❑ Set the correct expectations of your course?
- ❑ Have fewer than 60 characters?

STEP FIVE: TALK ABOUT WHY THIS COURSE IS A GUARANTEED GAME-CHANGER

You can include all the flashy sales jargon you want on your course's sales page but one thing remains true: People don't buy your course; they buy the results you promise.

Take your market research along with your target audience profile (client avatar/ideal client) and start jotting down ways your course will change them or transform their lives.

Now try weaving one of those benefits into your course name. When your ideal client reads your course name, they should know that course is meant for them and they should know what you're promising, or how their life will be transformed.

Which course name stands out more: "How to Start a Podcast" or "How to Host a Podcast That Turn Followers Into Lifelong Fans"?

That first choice is straightforward and to the point: You know what you're getting. But does it capture your attention? Does it stand out from the other 500 courses all about starting a podcast?

Now take the second choice, "How to Host a Podcast That Turn Followers Into Lifelong Fans" Even if you already have a podcast, you know right away that you'll learn hosting tips for making your podcast so exciting that your fans will sing your praises from the mountain tops... and who doesn't want that result?

That excitement the buyer feels when they think of all the lifelong fans they'll acquire is the emotional response you want your course name to evoke. An emotional reaction will encourage them to buy your course because they desperately want the results and transformation that you're promising.

If you're not sure how to elicit an emotional response through your copy, check out this list of 401+ Power Words Below:

BEAUTY	LUST	GRAVITY	SADNESS	SIMPLICITY
Adorable	Begging	Gargantuan	Alarming	Basic
Awe-Inspiring	Crave	Gigantic	Crushing	Cheat-Sheet
Beautiful	Decadent	Huge	Dead	Easy
Breathtaking	Delirious	Intense	Deceptive	Effortless
Dazzling	Fantasy	Massive	Devastating	Ingredients
Gorgeous	Forbidden	Gripping	Excruciating	Minimalist
Stunning	Irresistible	Goddamn	Exposed	On-Demand
Swoon	Naked	Seriously	Heartbreaking	Painless
Swoon-worthy	Provocative		Sadly	Rules
	Seductive		Shaming	Savvy
INDULGENCE	Sexy		Suffer	Simple
Guilt	Sinful		Avoid	Step-by-Step
Guilt-free	Tantalizing		Demoralizing	Stupid-simple
Indulgent	Satisfy		Problem	Tricks
Obsessed				Tweaks
Ravenous				
Lazy				

COMPLETENESS	GREED	SAVAGERY	NOVELTY	AUTHORITY
Completely	Affordable	Agonizing	Challenge	Absolute
Copy	Bargain	Apocalypse	Discover	All-Inclusive
Detailed	Barrage	Armageddon	Extraordinary	Authentic
Essential	Bonus	Battle	Hack	Authoritative
Impenetrable	Budget	Corrupt	Latest	Authority
Meticulous	Cheap	Crazy	Life-changing	Backed
Overcome	Convert	Deadly	Magic	Bona fide
Painstaking	Double	Disgusting	Miracle	Complete
Practical	Drive	Fight	New	Comprehensive
Recreate	Forever	Frenzy	Remarkable	Conclusive
Replicate	Free	Hate	Revolutionary	Definitive
Relentless	Immediately	Insane	Sensational	Document
Ultimate	Increase	Lunatic	Shocking	Expert
Master	Instantly	Menacing	Spoiler	Final
Perfect	Money	Painful	Startling	Formula
Super	Never	Poison	Suddenly	Genuine
Create	Now	Rowdy	Surprising	Guaranteed
Step-by-Step	Off-limits	Sabotaging	Unexpected	Honest
Best	Overnight	Savage	Strange	Iron-clad
Truly	Profit	Sins	Weird	Legitimate
Packed	Promote	Struggle	Odd	Literally
Extremely	Sale	Treacherous	Unusual	Official
Deep	Today	Uncontrollable		Powerful
Better	Triple	Vicious		Proven
	Unlimited	Violent	IMPATIENCE	Psychological
	Envy	Weak	Amp	Reliable
EXCITEMENT	Master	Wild	Blast	Report
Bold	Lucrative	Dying	Ignite	Research
Exciting	Steal	Horrifying	Jumpstart	Results
Fascinating		Attack	Kickstart	Solution
Intriguing		Traumatized	Launch	Strategy
Riveting		Insult	Quick-start	Studies
Tempting		Horribly	Speedy	Surefire
Thrilling		Hell	Supercharge	Validate
Transform			Turbo-charge	Masterclass
			Smuggle	

MEMORABILITY	SAFETY	PRIDE	EXCLUSIVITY	MIND-BLOWING
Captivate	Accuse	Absurd	Admit	Alluring
Genius	Assault	Achieve	Breaking	Amazing
Memorable	Beware	Awkward	Confess	Astonishing
Undeniable	Broke	Blunder	Confession	Astounding
Unforgettable	Catastrophe	Clueless	Divulge	Awesome
Unpopular	Caution	Cringeworthy	Elite	Badass
Impressive	Cheat	Dumb	Emerging	Bomb
Embarrassing	Dangerous	Fail	First	Brilliant
	Diagnosed	Fail-Proof	Hidden	Catapult
	Dirty	Failure	Insider	Charming
HUMOR	Emergency	Faux Pas	Little-known	Defying
Funniest	Ethical	Fool	New	Delicious
Hilarious	Exactly	Foolish	Popular	Delightful
Laugh	Fierce	Idiot	Priceless	Dreamy
Ridiculous	Hoax	Lame	Rare	Epic
	Horror	Last	Release	Explosive
	Jeopardy	Mediocre	Reveal	Exquisite
PRESTIGE	Lifetime	Mistake	Secret	Greatness
Expensive	Protect	Obvious	Sly	Heavenly
Glamorous	Provoke	Pitiful	Sneak-Peek	Incredible
Luxurious	Punch	Reject	Sneaky	Jaw-dropping
	Recession-Proof	Rookie	Special	Kickass
HAPPINESS	Sacred	Ruin	Stealthy	Legendary
Heartwarming	Safe	Senseless	Trend	Mesmerizing
Inspiring	Scam	Shameful	Truth	Mouth-watering
Profound	Scared	Silly	Unadulterated	Nail
Zen	Shaking	Stupid	Unconventional	Spellbinding
Alive	Signs	Success	Uncovered	Sublime
Light	Survive	Threaten	Undercover	Triumph
Healthy	Terrifying	Triggers	Underused	Unbelievable
	Unstoppable	Unknowingly	Unique	Unleashed
	Belong	Useless	Unseen	Polarizing
	Promise	Waste	Untapped	Dominate
	Stop		Worst	

EXERCISE: Think about how your course will change or transform your students' lives.

What are the benefits of my course?		
What will my students:	BEFORE my course	AFTER my course
HAVE		
FEEL		
KNOW		
WANT/DESIRE		

What Emotion(s) Suits My Course?	Favorite Power Words

STEP SIX: BETA-TEST YOUR COURSE WITH YOUR FRIENDS AND FAM

Even if you think you have the perfect name for your course, test it out with some friends and family before you start creating graphics and implementing a full marketing campaign. Remember, just because YOU love the name doesn't mean your target audience will love it, and who is this course for?

Who should you ask for opinions? That choice is up to you but there are a few groups of people who will give you different results.

1. Friends and family. These people will likely give you encouragement that your course name sounds great but if you want to dig deeper, ask them specific questions.

"Who do you think is the ideal student for this course? Does this name evoke emotion? If so, how did it make you feel?"

2. Business peers. These other business owners are in your networking circle in real life and online.

They will look at your course name with a business eye that is more critical than your friends and family.

They will also likely give you more constructive feedback and suggestions, especially if they have experience with this type of product creation.

3. Your target audience. Create a short poll for your target audience and invite them to give you feedback.

Your questions can be as simple as, "Which name excites you more, Choice A or Choice B?" Not only are you doing research but you're creating buzz about your new course.

If you're brave, create a Facebook poll on your business page, within your group, or within other groups in which you participate (provided it doesn't go against group rules) and see which name gets the most votes.

Sometimes we need that outside input when we're so close to the project ourselves.

Also, consider running a beta test for the whole course once you're done tweaking your course name. A beta test is simply a test run of the entire process, from making the purchase of the course to accessing the lessons.

Consider asking a couple of business peers or friends to run the process for you in exchange for feedback about any problems they encounter or questions they have specifically about the content.

A few lucky people in your target market can also serve as beta testers by going through the whole course and providing feedback.

Some beta groups receive the course for free while others pay a lower fee to participate. That choice is completely up to you and may depend on who your target market is.

Whatever feedback you receive, use it wisely to adjust the course and/or the name. Your reputation depends upon you presenting a killer product so listen to your market and make it the best.

Exercise: Make a plan of who will be your beta testers and how you'll solicit feedback.

Which names are my favorites?
1.
2.
3.

Who will I ask for feedback?	How will I ask for feedback?
1.	❑ Survey (SurveyMonkey.com)
2.	❑ Facebook poll on business page
	❑ Email my list asking questions or link to survey
3.	❑ Create my own in-person focus group
4.	
5.	

Beta Testers for My Course	
Who will I ask for feedback?	**How will I ask for feedback?**
1.	❑ Survey (SurveyMonkey.com)
	❑ Facebook poll on business page
2.	❑ Email my list asking questions or
	link to survey
3.	❑ Create my own in-person
	focus group
4.	❑ Set a deadline!
5.	

Simple Thank You Gift Ideas

Consider offering a simple thank you gift for participating in your survey or focus group. Don't over think it and don't make it so large or expensive (such as a big discount on packages) that you lose money.

1.

2.

3.

4.

5.

Feedback Results	
Group 1	**Specific Comments**
Who is in this group?	
Group 2	**Specific Comments**
Who is in this group?	

SURVEY RESULTS

Take note of all the responses, even negative feedback. Use all these results to tweak your course and its name as needed.

5/15 - Coaching Your Tribe with Your Principles (Live Coaching)

When I first started my business, I loved doing one on one coaching and I still do but as I got busier, and my time became more limited I needed a way to reach more people at an affordable price for them. Live Coaching Programs was the Win-Win solution. Not only was I able to give my clients my time at an affordable price, I also got rewarded because there isn't a cap on how many people can join. This allowed me to continue to give value in a group setting because people can easily learn from other's questions, and it also allowed my income to continue to grow on a monthly basis. Live Coaching Programs can also be done virtually which brings your overhead down as well. This is easy to do with Zoom for as little as $15 a month or even Google Meets. They can connect with their phone, tablet, or computer. You can even record the session and send the video to clients who had to miss it.

To create a live coaching program based on your book you need to do the following steps below:

Step 1: Identify Your Theme

If you wrote your book correctly then you already have the one promise you are giving your reader and potential coaching participants but if not make sure your theme aligns with your book. Answer these questions to find clarity on what your group coaching program is about:

1. What is your expertise as a coach? I.e., Wealth, Health, Mindset, Productivity, Spirituality, etc.

_____

_____

_____

_____

_____

_____

_____

_____

_____

_____

_____

_____

_____

_____

_____

_____

2. What are the results you want to help people achieve? This will
    determine the clients you choose for your program because
    you want the RIGHT people to coach in order to get a high
    finish and success rate. Make sure your results are S.M.A.R.T.
    = Specific, Measurable, Achievable, Relatable, and Time for
    Example, I help authors generate 6-7 figures in 12 months from
    their book.

_____

_____

_____

_____

_____

_____

_____

_____

_____

_____

_____

_____

_____

_____

_____

3. Why do you want to start a group coaching program? Money
    should NOT be the only answer! Getting clear on your WHY
    is imperative because it will assure that you are fully vested in
    your group's success.

_____

_____

_____

_____

_____

_____

_____

_____

_____

_____

_____

_____

_____

_____

_____

_____

_____

_____

Step 2: Create Your Group Coaching Framework

Having selected a program theme, you're now ready to begin thinking about the group coaching framework, which includes program length and delivery time. As far as how lengthy (or short) a group coaching program should be, there aren't any hard and fast rules. It's better to choose a long program than a short one though. Here's the reason... Creating a program that is too short or too condensed will rob your participants of the opportunity to do the work, take action, and start seeing results, which is why coaching groups is an art more than a science. Think about putting together a three-month-long group program. It's common for group coaching programs to last for six months or even longer. You should also think about HOW your group coaching program will be delivered. As an example, you may test a subscription model in which clients pay a monthly fee to continue working with you in a group program. You may want to consider a yearly charge at an acceptable pricing point to encourage clients to commit for longer periods of time if this sounds appealing.

A yearly fee in a subscription model is great for 2 reasons:

1. You get paid upfront for the whole year and this is an effective way to secure stable income in your business.
2. Since your clients paid a significant amount upfront, they'll be motivated to see the program through and do the work to get their desired results.

You can also create a month-to-month structure, but you are more likely to have people drop off it you go that route. Use the space below to determine your framework:

1. Do you prefer working with people over a longer period or do you like working with fresh faces as often as possible?

_____

_____

_____

_____

_____

_____

_____

_____

_____

_____

_____

_____

_____

2. Have you experienced group coaching as a client? If yes, what was the timeframe? Did you think it was too short, too long or just right? Why?

_____

_____

_____

_____

_____

_____

_____

_____

_____

_____

_____

_____

_____

_____

_____

_____

_____

_____

_____

_____

_____

_____

3. Based on your group coaching theme (the one you chose in
   Step 1), how long should your program be for members to start
   seeing results? Don't Overthink this! Go with what feels right.

_____

_____

_____

_____

_____

_____

_____

_____

_____

_____

_____

_____

_____

_____

_____

_____

Would a subscription model work for you and your business? Are you going to implement month, quarterly, or annual renewals?

_____

_____

_____

_____

_____

_____

_____

_____

_____

_____

_____

_____

_____

_____

_____

_____

Step 3: Implement Accountability into Your Program

Creating an accountability portion of your program will increase the completion rate and help get you, new participants, via testimonials and word of mouth. Use the space below to determine which direction you desire to go:

1. Which accountability model speaks to you? Is it small break-out groups of 3 to 5 people? Partnerships with 2 people? Each member reporting to the entire group? If none of these sound good, what other ways can you creatively include accountability in your group?

_____

_____

_____

_____

_____

_____

_____

_____

_____

_____

_____

_____

_____

_____

_____

_____

_____

2. How do you plan to stay involved? Do you want to check in on individual breakout groups and partnerships every couple of days, once a week, a couple of times a month?

_____

_____

_____

_____

_____

_____

_____

_____

_____

_____

_____

_____

_____

_____

_____

_____

_____
_____
_____
_____
_____
_____

3. List out any other ideas you have around creating accountability in your group.

_____
_____
_____
_____
_____
_____
_____
_____
_____
_____
_____
_____
_____
_____
_____
_____
_____
_____

Step 4: Build Trust

As a group coach, trust is essential because it creates a safe environment in which each participant can learn at their own pace. We need trust as a glue to keep our group together, so think of it like that.

Communication, involvement, and connection within and between members of a group suffer when there is a lack of trust. Building trust takes time, and that's the first thing you should know about it. Keep in mind that while some group members may be familiar with YOU, the rest of the group may include people you've never met before. So, don't force yourself into it, and don't push it.

Spend some time connecting the group's members and promoting interaction both within and outside the group. Asking "ice-breaker" questions can help build trust among the members of the group right from the start, allowing them to feel a strong sense of community from the get-go.

At the beginning of a group coaching course, great questions can help build and strengthen trust.

Here are some ice-breaker questions to get your group talking and building trust:

1. What are your personal values?
2. What is your biggest goal in this program and why did you choose this goal?
3. If you could have everyone else in the group know one important thing about you, what would it be?

4. Where did you grow up and what was it like growing up in your hometown?
5. What's your favorite movie/book/song of all time?
6. If you could invite 3 people to a "dream dinner party," who would they be?

Step 5: Keep Your Group Engaged

Lastly keeping your group engaged is important to keep the momentum of the group and increase it's value. You want your group to get more than they bargained for in your program and you want them to sing your praises to their network.

Use the space below to create your engagement:

1. How many people would you like to have in your group program?

_____

_____

_____

_____

_____

_____

_____

_____

_____

_____

_____

_____

_____

_____

2. How do you want to increase engagement? Think about mini contests, freebies and surprise bonuses you can include to keep things interesting.

_____

_____

_____

_____

_____

_____

_____

_____

_____

_____

_____

_____

_____

_____

_____

_____

_____

3. What's the price of your program? This is a big question so don't feel like you have to answer right away. Set aside a couple of hours this week to research pricing on group coaching programs in your industry and niche before settling on a price or a price range that's right for you.

_____

_____

_____

_____

_____

_____

_____

_____

_____

_____

_____

_____

_____

_____

_____

_____

_____

_____

_____

_____

_____

6/15 – Duplicating Yourself and Your Message (Certificate Program)

One of the smartest ways to increase your influence, impact, and income is to certify other people to speak, coach, and train on your content.

Once you create a framework and methodology for what you are teaching, creating a program to teach others how to help others get the results you promise will help to continue to grow your brand and influence.

A certificate program is almost like franchising a business because whoever is being certified is using your experience and content to start something that will also be lucrative to them.

Below is a guide to help you to figure out what are the things you need to do before you launch your certificate program:

1. Build Brand Awareness

No one is really going to be excited about joining your certificate program if your brand doesn't have equity. If no one knows who you or your brand is or if it isn't easy to do research and find your brand online, then your certificate program won't have a lot of value. People like to connect themselves with brands that are already established so it is important that you make yourself the authority in your space.

2. Cultivate A Community

Who better to be certified in your program than those who are already loyal fans of your work? It is imperative that you cultivate a build a strong community in order to have those in your tribe be the first cohorts of your work. This will help your certificate program grow exponentially as others will see how dedicated your people are and will want to join a tribe of movers and shakers.

3. Build Authority / Thought Leadership

Building authority or thought leadership in a specific field or industry requires a combination of expertise, credibility, and visibility. Here are a few steps you can take to build your authority and establish yourself as a thought leader:

1. Develop a deep understanding of your field or industry: Stay up-to-date with the latest research, trends, and developments in your area of expertise. Read industry publications, attend conferences and networking events, and join professional organizations.

2. Share your expertise: Share your knowledge and insights through various channels such as writing blog posts, creating videos, podcasting, or speaking at events. Share your expertise on social media platforms like LinkedIn, Twitter, and Facebook.

3. Create valuable content: Create valuable, high-quality content that educates, entertains, and informs your target audience. This will help to establish you as a credible source of information and a thought leader in your field.

4. Network and collaborate: Network with other experts and thought leaders in your field. Collaborate on projects and share resources and knowledge. This will help you to expand your reach and gain visibility.

5. Measure and track your progress: Track your progress by measuring key metrics such as website traffic, social media engagement, and email subscribers. Use this data to refine your strategy and improve your efforts over time.

6. Be consistent: Building authority takes time and consistency. You need to consistently produce valuable content, engage with your audience, and position yourself as an expert in your field.

In a nutshell, these steps will make you an authority in your space and as discussed above building authority and thought leadership will enhance your brand awareness so people will be willing to follow your advice and methodologies. Authority and Thought leadership is also important because without it someone can easily try to mimic your content and pass it off as their own.

7/15 - MAKING SURE THEY HEAR YOU CLEARLY (KEYNOTE SPEAKING)

When I began my journey as a financial educator after retiring from Banking, my goal was to spread my ideology as far and wide as possible. I started out doing local talks at churches, and schools but eventually I needed to get on big stages to spread my message faster. Keynote speaking as an author not only allowed me to sell books faster but also gave me exponential growth because those who heard me speak would talk about me to their friends and family. Also now with social media, big talks make great content for social.

Did I mention that you will get paid to spread your message? This is a win-win because you are the authority on the subject… and you authored the book on it too! You should be the one to talk about what you know best. In addition, as an added bonus keynote speakers frequently visit stunning locations and meet fascinating individuals as part of their work.

Below is a guide that is going to help you get your first speaking gig as an author:

1. Identify Your Ideal Audience

The secret to a successful speaking engagement is simple: offer content that is both interesting and useful to the audience. Once you're able to do that, it becomes a lot easier to secure engagements.

The initial step in securing speaking engagements has nothing to do with event planners, speakers bureaus, or PR; You should focus on identifying your target market first. Who do you want to talk to? And why?

Don't make the mistake that most authors make when they first start out speaking… Rather than focusing on the small, loyal audience, they should serve, many Authors are distracted by the biggest or most prominent stages.

Let me be clear: Getting a five-figure speaking fee for a presentation at YouTube's corporate headquarters is fantastic, but unless YouTube provides the entryway to your desired audience, you shouldn't focus on their platform for your business. Your goals should always be tied to who your target audience is.

If you want to increase your client base, you should speak at conferences that your ideal customers are likely to attend. Again, the first step in securing speaking engagements is to know exactly who you're speaking to and why your message is important to them.

2. Identify Your Ideal Speaking Gigs

Now that you know your ideal audience, it's time to think about ways to get in front of them by choosing the right speaking engagements. Are you looking for small-scale events with book signings, or are you looking for large-scale events with executives and a lot of people?

What's the best possible way to get your message out to the people you want to reach? It's a good idea to select 25 or 30 people who are exactly like your target demographic. These are the kinds of people you want to meet through your speaking engagements in the long term. What are their top picks for events this year?

Once you have this data, start looking at those events and ask yourself, "What are they looking for when they hire speakers?" Remember, it's not only about what speaking engagement fits what you're looking for; you also have to be a good fit for them as well.

Anything is possible, so ALWAYS stay ready! You shouldn't expect to be on the TED main stage with your first book, but you never know. If you're in energetic alignment, you'll be able to perform at large venues right away, but for the majority, it takes years to establish a solid foundation and gain entry.

3. Choose Your Topic

Next, it's time to choose a topic. You've got the book, so you've got all the information you need to put a powerful talk together. Even so, you'll need to narrow down your talk's content to something that can be covered in a 30, 45, or 60-minute slot.

You can use this topic to show off your expertise while also addressing current challenges that your audience may be facing. Give your viewers the facts. Tell them a tale. Give them instances of what you're talking about. Get your hands dirty. Don't forget to provide the audience with specific steps they can take to achieve what you've promised.

Also, think about how you're going to say it. Does the subject matter lend itself to a good joke? Is this a difficult topic that necessitates you to simplify and explain it in detail? Decide how you are going to approach it and stay consistent.

4. Create Your Speaker's Press Kit

A Speaker's Press Kit is necessary to give people who will potentially book you for a speech a quit snapshot of who you are and what you plan to bring to the table.

It's a single, professionally designed PDF file that includes:

- a list of your impressive past speaking experiences (the top 5-10 stages you've spoken on)
- testimonials that give proof of the impact you can make on an audience
- links or blurbs from any media you've been featured in

The purpose of a press kit is to persuade and impress the organizer of the event. In other words, if you can't produce a visually pleasing and professional-looking PDF, don't bother creating it at all.

Please see next page for an example of my professional press kit:

Ash Cash Exantus

Helping People Live Their Best Financial Lives

Personal Finance Expert • Wealth Coach • 4x Best Selling Author

WORK WITH ASH

SPEAKING
- Keynotes
- Panel Discussion
- Break-Out Sessions & Workshops
- Corporate Training
- Moderator and VIP event host

PRESS + MEDIA
- Television
- Radio
- RMT / SMT
- Print

PARTNERSHIP
- Spokesperson
- Brand Ambassador
- Influencer Programs and campaigns

Features

Sharing his bold positivity and knack for empowering people financially, Ash has spoken and written for the following platforms and media outlets.

FOX BUSINESS — CNN Money — msnbc.com — AMERICAN BANKER — CRAIN'S

WSJ — NY1 — HUFFPOST — The New York Times — Newsday

PIX11 NEWS — POPSUGAR — U.S.News — BLACK ENTERPRISE — YAHOO! FINANCE

CNBC — USA TODAY — iHeart RADIO — Forbes — SiriusXM

TODAY — BET★ — iHeart RADIO — BUSTLE — URBAN ONE

CONTACT

Email: AmcenasMindRightMoney.com   **Phone:** 877.740.7240 (office)   646.687.4152 (Text)

Who is Ash Exantus?

@IamAshCash

Ash Exantus aka Ash Cash is a 15-year banking executive, personal finance expert, motivational speaker, and the author of six books, including three Amazon.com bestsellers. He is the founder and Chief Financial Educator at MindRight Money Management, a Financial Education and Media company that blends psychology and personal finance with music, pop culture and relevant news to help people manage their money better in order to live the life that they want.

Ash has established himself as a thought leader and trusted voice with Corporate America, Colleges, Churches, and Community based organizations. Through his message of fiscal responsibility, entrepreneurship, and wealth empowerment, he has become a regular speaker at national conferences across the country. Ash has been featured on popular, national media outlets such as CNN, The New York Times, WSJ, American Banker, CNBC, TheStreet.com, Black Enterprise, USA Today, Forbes, BET, Pix11 Morning News, and countless others.

Above all of his credentials, accolades, and titles, Ash is simply known for helping people maximize their full potentials. You can also read more about Ash by visiting www.IamAshCash.com.

250K

Social
Media
Followers

Podcast
Download

E-mail
Subscribers

Audience

49% Men

51% Women

25-54 Years Old

CONTACT

Email: Ameena@MindRightMoney.com   Phone: 877.740.7240 (office)   646.687.4152 (Text)   2

5. Create a Speaker's Reel

A speaker's reel is a short video that showcases your unique style and stage presence on the microphone. Organizers will have more faith in your ability to hold an audience's attention when you have demonstrated your expertise.

Your speaker's reel can help event planners decide if you're a good fit for their conference or event. This is advantageous to both you and the target audience in the long run.

The content and tone of your talk should reflect your Author brand. For your speaking reel, the same holds true. An accurate portrayal of your personality and abilities should be conveyed in your speaking reel.

Make yourself what you want to be, not what you think others want to see. Showcase your personality and believe that event planners will make the best decisions for their audience when searching for engagements.

Please see the link below for an example of my speaker's reel:

https://youtu.be/lww3ip1O1PM

6. Figure out Who to Contact

Begin reaching out to potential speaking engagements as soon as your materials are ready. Many events offer online forms that you can fill out, but if you can find the correct person to contact, your pitch will be stronger. In comparison to a generic "to whom it may concern," an email addressed to a specific person has a much greater impact.

Take a look at LinkedIn to see if there is a meeting planner who can help you with your top 20-30 events. Start by looking around for the conference's name or logo. Enter "event" or "event manager" in the search filter.

A Google search for "brand name plus event plus press release" or "event plus year plus press release" should yield results if the previous method fails. This should lead to a potential business contact directly for the event. In order to find out the email address of the person you're looking for, try Hunter IO or Rocket Reach.

7. CREATE YOUR PITCH

Now it's time to put together your email. The following are questions to ask yourself?

1. What challenges does this organization face when looking to hire a speaker?

2. When looking for a speaker, what keywords do they type into Google?

Use these challenges and keywords in your email.

Do not be vague or ambiguous. Emails like these should be brief. There is no need to go into detail about your skills, abilities, or subject matter in order to get them interested.

Provide a list of actionable takeaways for the intended audience to follow. What are the benefits of attending this presentation? And why is it critical to them that they get these takeaways? Using this list, you can demonstrate that you have a thorough understanding of the event and its participants.

Make sure to include a brief description of your achievements. Include no more than two or three of the most noteworthy items. Attach the press kit. Include a link to a video of your speaker's reel. Attaching a video may lead your email to be marked as spam or cause the recipient's inbox to become overburdened, so ONLY provide a link.

8. BUILD REAL RELATIONSHIPS!

Don't swarm 50 people with a pitch. The key to securing speaking engagements is cultivating a network of contacts. Prior to sending a pitch to the right 10-15 people, spend some time getting to know each other.

Like and comment on their social media posts. Send them articles you think they'll enjoy. Be as courteous as possible in order to help them feel seen and appreciated.

Sales cold calls rarely get anyone to buy anything. This is because they are impersonal. Booking speaking engagements are the same way. If you have a personal relationship with the event planner, you will be a more appealing prospect.

They're looking for someone who can establish a rapport with their target audience and offer insightful commentary. They are looking for a person.

9. DON'T BE TOO PUSHY

Show initiative, but don't go overboard when you're ready to deliver your pitch. To avoid getting your IP address blacklisted, you should limit yourself to one email at a time. Nobody likes being pushed, bullied, or annoyed.

Here's how you should proceed:

1. Send your first email.
2. If you don't get a response, follow up 2 days later.
3. If you still don't hear anything, follow up one week after that.
4. Try a final follow-up one week after that.

The fourth email should be your final email. Include a sentence such as, "I haven't heard back from you, so I presume you aren't interested. I won't reach out again, but please let me know if anything changes." Unless you've got something new to say, don't keep pitching the same thing over and over again.

10. Determine Your Speaking Fee

Most likely, you won't be compensated for your first professional speaking gigs. This is because most paying gigs would prefer to see you speak prior to paying you, so if you don't have footage of your talk (Since you're just getting started), you have to use the connections you already have. Let people know you'd be interested in giving speeches and see what happens.

Consider this stage of your speaking career to be a sort of internship. In a sense, you're creating a portfolio. Eventually, you'll be able to earn money through speaking engagements. Some events pay more than others, and this varies according to the "stage."

You hear about professional speakers charging thousands of dollars because they've worked their way up to a specific degree of expertise in public speaking. As a result, they're in high demand and tend to avoid the pitching process altogether.

Talks are a great method to spread the word about your business, products, and services. You can use them to get the word out about your abilities and broaden your reach so getting paid to speak is a win-win for your impact AND income!

8/15 – Corporations Pay for Your Influence (Content Marketing)

Once you make yourself the AUTHORity with your Book, there will be many companies and brands that are a natural fit for your audience. For example, when I wrote the book, "What the FICO: 12 Steps to Repairing Your Credit." Credit repair companies, credit bureaus, and credit card companies who offered secured credit cards were natural partners for me. This allowed me to promote my book and also get paid to be a spokesperson for a company that aligns with my message.

Often referred to as a brand ambassador, a corporate ambassador or an influencer, this person is a professional who promotes a company and its products or services. A brand ambassador's job is to spread the word about a company's products or services to the public. Celebrities used to be the primary public brand ambassadors, but today anyone can become an influencer and get money doing so.

In addition to performing marketing efforts, brand ambassadors can also post about a product on social media or represent a firm at a trade fair.

Below are 6 steps to becoming a brand ambassador

1. Find Brands that Align with You and Your Message

Start by researching the companies you're considering. A company's principles, personality, and brand should all be taken into consideration when you as an influencer are looking to work with them.

Get a feel of what a company is looking for as a brand ambassador by looking at their social media posts and researching their current influencers. You should look for brands that represent your interests or that relate to the content you already provide. Remember; to become an official brand ambassador for a company or organization, you may need to endorse them publicly, so make sure you are aligned with their brand message.

2. Engage with Your Social Media Followers

Engaging with your followers on social media—by getting likes and comments—is a terrific way of promoting yourself as an ideal candidate to be a company's brand ambassador. Social media is a great place to start, but it's also a great place to grow your audience. Having a significant number of social media likes and comments raises your profile in the eyes of possible clients.

Commenting on well-known pages and blogs will help you gain more followers as well. It's also a good idea to respond to the messages and comments you get on your own social media profiles.

3. Define Your Online Personality and Image

Many brand ambassadors have a distinct online identity that they use to promote their products. The tone, appearance, and interests of your social media posts should all be consistent. If you want to show off a special interest, such as a love for art or a particular kind of music, you may want to style your outfit in a specific way or take images that reflect that. In the long term, companies search for brand ambassadors who embody a certain image.

4. Connect with Your Followers

Encourage your followers, as well as others you meet, to share their own experiences, ask questions, write comments, and answer as many as you possibly can. Meet your fans in person when safely possible; you can conduct meetups in public places like a cafe or shopping center. The more personal and dynamic your social media profiles are, the more followers you will attract, and the more engaged your current followers will be.

5. Focus on Growth

Boost your social media presence by gaining more subscriptions and followers. To supplement your in-person marketing activities, you can promote your attendance at select events, encourage others to join, and cultivate a greater online following. Connect with other social media influencers in order to grow your own audience. As a brand ambassador, the more followers you have who interact with the brand, the more money you will make.

6. CONTACT RELEVANT BRANDS

Once you've found the kind of brands you would like to work with, start reaching out to them to see what kind of ambassadors they are looking for.

You could reach out to the company's social media accounts and inquire about the prospect of serving as their Brand Ambassador. They might respond with more information if they're interested.

For face-to-face possibilities, look up upcoming events in your neighborhood. At one of these gatherings, make contact with a company's representatives.

9/15 – Taking Your Show on the Road (Live Events)

Your book is both a message and a catalyst for change. Neither you nor your book should be underestimated. Those who are fortunate enough to cross your path will gladly pay to gain access to both you and your book. You can expand your reach, impact, and income by doing live events.

You can do live events on your own, hire a team to assist you or enlist the help of volunteers. However, as someone who has participated in numerous live events, I can attest that they are not for the faint of heart. As a result, I recommend hiring a professional to assist you, whether it be to oversee the event or to ensure that everything is organized and carried out correctly.

Whether you decide to run the event on your own or hire an expert, below is a checklist you should use to assure that your live event runs smoothly

4-6 MONTHS AHEAD OF EVENT

- ☐ Establish your event goals and objectives.
- ☐ Select the date.
- ☐ Identify venue and negotiate details.
- ☐ Develop an event master plan.
- ☐ Get cost estimates. Some costs you might need to consider are:
  - o Room rental
  - o Food and beverages
  - o Equipment
  - o Speaker fees
  - o Travel for staff
  - o Insurance
- ☐ Create an event budget.
- ☐ Recruit an event committee. This includes selecting an event manager or chair and establishing sub-committee chairs.
- ☐ Brand your event.
  - o Start building out an event website or pages on your website that describe the event.
  - o Develop an event logo and tagline.

- ☐ Create and launch publicity plan. This includes ensuring staff and/or volunteers are identified to manage specific tasks – e.g., media relations, VIP coordination, printed material design & printing coordination, signage, online /social media, etc.
- ☐ Identify and confirm speakers/presenters/entertainers.
- ☐ Identify and contact sponsors/partners.
- ☐ Determine if you need event registration software to make the process easier.
- ☐ Determine if you need other event management software.
- ☐ Release early-bird tickets.
    - o Ensure registration forms are accessible and allow space for preferred pronouns and preferred names.

3-4 MONTHS AHEAD OF EVENT

☐ Build out required documents for your team.

☐ Speaker/presenter/entertainer liaison:

    o Finalize presentation/speech topics

    o Get bio information, photo

    o Travel & accommodation arrangements

    o Have contracts signed if appropriate

    o Ask speakers to start promoting and sharing it with their network

☐ Financial/Administration:

    o Determine registration fees

    o Set up and enable online registration

    o Finalize sponsor levels and amounts

    o Identify items to be underwritten and accounting tracking details

☐ Venue and logistics planning:

    o Determine and arrange all details re menu, A/V equipment, registration set-up, parking, signage, etc.

    o Review security needs/plan for the event with venue manager

    o Investigate need for any special permits, licenses, insurance, etc.

    o Assess accessibility requirements (e.g. all-gender restrooms, wheelchair accessibility, etc).

    o Communicate accessibility requirements to staff.

- ☐ Follow publicity plan:
  - o Develop draft program
  - o Create draft event script (e.g., MC, speaker introductions, thanks, closing, etc.)
  - o Develop publicity pieces -- e.g., newsletter articles and/or ads, radio spots, print blog posts articles for submission to other publications and/or ads, etc.
  - o Request logos from corporate sponsors for online and printed materials
  - o Develop and produce invitations, programs, posters, tickets, etc.
  - o Develop media list & prepare News Release, Media Advisory, Backgrounder and all media kit materials (e.g., speaker info, photos, etc.)
  - o Create event page on your website
  - o Enable/create email event notifications
  - o Create a Facebook event page
  - o Develop a promo video and post on YouTube and your Facebook page
  - o Register your event on a variety of online event calendars
  - o Create some buzz on your blog or member forums
  - o Determine VIPs and create invitation & tracking document (e.g., spreadsheet)
  - o Order any desired event swag

1-2 MONTHS AHEAD OF EVENT

- ☐ Send reminders to your contact list regarding registration and participation.
- ☐ Reach out again to presenters/speakers regarding:
    - ○ Confirming travel and accommodation details
    - ○ Request copy of speeches and/or presentations
- ☐ Sponsorship finalization:
    - ○ Follow up to confirm sponsorships and underwriting
    - ○ Get any promotional materials you'll be sharing at the event
    - ○ Ask sponsors to share event on their promotional channels
- ☐ Continue executing on your publicity plan:
    - ○ Release press announcements about keynote speakers, celebrities, VIPs attending, honorees, etc.
    - ○ Post your initial event news release on your website and circulate to all partners, affiliated organizations, etc.
    - ○ Post more details about your event on social media
- ☐ Close early-bird tickets; release standard pricing.
- ☐ Finalize and proofread printed materials.

1 WEEK AHEAD OF EVENT

- ☐ Have all committee chairs meet and confirm all details against Master Plan. You should also ensure back-up plans are developed for any situation (e.g., back-up volunteers as VIP greeters, additional volunteers for registration or set-up, etc)
- ☐ Finalize event script.
  - o Assign practice sessions for anyone who has a speaking slot.
- ☐ Brief any/all hosts, greeters, volunteers about their event duties and timelines.
- ☐ Finalize your seating plan.
  - o Ensure it includes wheelchair-accessible areas and has clear paths through the venue.
- ☐ Provide final registration numbers to caterer.
- ☐ Make print and online copies of any speeches, videos, and presentations.
- ☐ Do a final registration check, including name badges & registration list. Depending on when your registration closes, this may not be possible until a few days in advance but try to finish it as early as possible.
- ☐ Determine photo op and interview opportunities with any presenters and VIPs.
- ☐ Confirm details with media attendees.

1 DAY BEFORE THE EVENT

- ☐ Confirm media attendance.
- ☐ Ensure all signage is in place — both around the venue and any other areas in which it's needed.
- ☐ Ensure registration and media tables are prepared and stocked with necessary items (such as blank name badges, paper, pens, tape, stapler, etc.)
  - o Ensure there are enough outlets. If not, consider bringing power bars for attendees and your team.
- ☐ Ensure all promo items, gifts, plaques, trophies, etc. are on-site.
- ☐ Ensure all A/V equipment is set up and working properly.
- ☐ Get a good night's sleep! You'll need the rest before the exciting day to come.

EVENT DAY

- ☐ Take a few deep breaths — you got this!
- ☐ Ensure you have copies of all instructions, directions, phone numbers, keys, extra parking permits for VIP guests, seating charts and guest lists with you
- ☐ Check in with each Committee Chair to ensure their team is on track.
  - o Also check in with catering and any sponsor teams that are attending.
- ☐ Assist sponsors, speakers, and other teams as needed.
- ☐ Greet new attendees.

POST EVENT FOLLOW-UP

While you need to conduct a thorough evaluation and update your budget, there are post- event publicity, fundraising and member development opportunities that you can take advantage of with just a little pre-event planning. Here are some of the activities you might consider once the event is over:

- ☐ Check in with venue. Ensure nothing important was left behind.
- ☐ Financial status:
    - o Gather all receipts and documentation, final registration data, etc.
    - o Update budget
- ☐ Send thank-you's and acknowledgement letters to:
    - o Sponsors
    - o Volunteers
    - o Speakers/presenters
    - o Donors
    - o The media

In your thank-you notes, be sure to remind the recipients of the event's success – and how they contributed (e.g., dollars raised, awareness - number of participants, etc.

☐ Post-event publicity:

  o Send out an email to your subscriber base with highlights from the event

  o Make a publicity reel video to share how it went (and as a bonus, you can use it as publicity next year!)

  o Share highlights on social media

  o Update website page to reflect that it's a past event.

☐ Conduct a post-event survey. Learn what people enjoyed about your event and where you have room to improve.

☐ Reach out to event participants. Thank them for participating and promote your ongoing programs and how they can support you throughout the year by joining, volunteering, or making a sustaining donation.

☐ Conduct a team debrief to learn their thoughts.

☐ Conduct a thorough evaluation of the event. What went well and what could you do better next time?

10/15 – COLLABORATING WITH OTHER THOUGHT LEADERS (CONFERENCES)

Conferences are similar to live events. Conferences are something that should never be attempted on one's own. The cost of hosting a conference will be determined by the size of the conference and the involvement of other speakers and event coordinators, but the benefit of conferences is that it allows you to invite other speakers and celebrities who can draw a large audience for your event. This is a big benefit because it exposes you to a new audience who can potentially become clients.

In the past, I've seen large-scale conferences with thousands of attendees, and they cost a lot of money. But on the flip side of that, as long as everything goes according to plan and the proper individuals are in place, it can be a rewarding endeavor.

Please refer to the previous chapter and use the worksheet if you are planning on creating your own conference, but again I HIGHLY suggest you hire a professional. Also, below is a list of conferences you should attend for education as well as to see the flow of a conference.

InkersCon*

Dallas, TX

InkersCon is run by Authors A.I. co-founder Alessandra Torre. Hundreds of authors will attend this gathering, which offers workshops and panels in writing, marketing, and business practices. The curriculum is designed to boost your career to the next level, whether you're starting out or an advanced author.

<u>Website: inkerscon.com</u>

SelfPub Con*

The Self-Publishing Advice Conference is run in association with the Alliance of Independent Authors (ALLi), the nonprofit professional association for self-published writers.

Website: selfpublishingadviceconference.com

Indy Romance Convention*

Lebanon, TN

The Indie Romance Convention is designed to fit the needs of indie authors. In addition, the event is open to readers, bloggers, editors and cover artists.

Website: indieromanceconvention.com

20Books Vegas*

Las Vegas, NV

20Books boasts the largest gathering of indie authors anywhere — likely north of 1,600 for this event. Much of the focus is on what it takes to make money as an independent author. Topics include making money, leveraging multiple revenue streams, social media, federal tax issues, business organization, and structure, plus more. This year's event moves to Bally's on the Strip.

Website: 20booksvegas.com

NINC Conference

TradeWinds resort in St. Pete Beach, Fla.

The Novelists, Inc. conference brings together multi-published, multi-genre authors who publish traditionally, independently or both. The speakers are selected from the top echelons of the industry and the conversations often rise above and beyond what you'll experience elsewhere.

Website: ninc.com

Digital Book World

Nashville, TN

Digital Book World is the gathering of the wide world of publishing. Trade, scholarly, independent, educational, corporate and many other types of publishing come together to share best practices and enjoy one-of-a-kind networking.

Website: digitalbookworld.com

11/15 - HELPING YOUR TRIBE ON A MONTHLY BASIS (SUBSCRIPTIONS)

As a financial educator, I preach residual income and passive income all day, which is the ability to get paid on a recurring basis for something of VALUE that you created once. Creating a subscription and/or membership program is the holy grail of the income you can receive as an author.

There are a wide range of options for running subscription or membership sites, including using a course platform you already know or are possibly using. If you return to Chapter 12, where we discuss self-study programs like online courses, you'll see that many of those programs also permit the creation of a membership site.

Imagine people paying you $17, $44, $97, or more per month to be part of the membership site based on your book. It might not sound impressive until you start crunching the numbers.

- 100 members at $17/mo is $20,400 annually
- 1,000 members at $17/mo is $204,000 annually
- 10,000 members at $17/mo is $2,040,000 annually
- 100 members at $44/mo is $52,800 annually
- 1,000 members at $44/mo is $528,000 annually
- 10,000 members at $44/mo is $5,280,000 annually
- 100 members at $97/mo is $116,400 annually
- 1,000 members at $97/mo is $1,164,000 annually
- 10,000 members at $97/mo is $11,640,000 annually

Subscription sites and membership sites are a simple yet powerful way to build community

Below is a checklist of things you need to consider while you are creating your membership or subscription service (This is a summary of the Book Oversubscribed which I HIGHLY suggest you read AND apply):

When you're oversubscribed, you're able to focus more on your current customers and less on finding new ones, which allows you to produce your best work.

As a result, you have more time to focus on product development rather than hawking your wares. Oversubscribed allows you to build your brand rather than blending in with the crowd.

7 Principles for Oversubscribed

PRINCIPLE #1 DEMAND AND SUPPLY SET THE PRICE.

"Why do businesses do well?" In a nutshell, they do so because of an increase in demand. There are three possible outcomes for your business based on demand:

1. Oversubscribed – demand is outstripping supply (result in profits)
2. Balanced – demand and supply are relatively even (result in wages, not profits)
3. Undersubscribed – excess supply is available above demand (result in losses)

PRINCIPLE #2 SEPARATE YOURSELF FROM THE MARKET.

Everyone isn't necessary for you to succeed. Fear of missing out is nothing to be afraid of. Be a one-stop shop for a select few. People who are truly interested in what you have to offer should be your customers. It's important to them that you produce results for them that they'll be proud of.

Be famous for a few. Here are key ingredients for being famous.

1. Consistent and repetitive message
2. Content
3. Commercial ecosystem
4. Continuity and visibility
5. Collaboration

PRINCIPLE #3 PAY ATTENTION TO THE FOUR DRIVERS OF MARKET IMBALANCE.

In order to create more buyers than sellers, there are four market imbalance drivers that you can use.

1. Innovation (innovate in terms of product, services, internal systems and your brand)
2. Relationships (do your best work and spend time with your current clients)
3. Convenience (find a unique distribution channel, automation and market information)
4. Price (invest, refine and systemize to lower costs)

PRINCIPLE #4 BUYING ENVIRONMENT CREATES BUYERS.

People do not purchase what others are trying to market. They buy what others desire to purchase. Never go out of your way to demonstrate how strongly you want to sell something. Your responsibility is to honor and hold in the highest regard the people who are already purchasing from you. If you do so, they will tell others what they purchased from you, and you will soon become oversubscribed.

"Treat your clients like they're celebrities and let them pull a crowd."

People do not purchase necessities. They purchase what they "want." Singapore, for instance, is one of the costliest destinations to purchase a Ferrari (about four times more than in the UK). Then why do so many individuals have them? The reason is because they 'want' one. It makes no difference how badly equipped or pricey the car is. What they 'desire' ultimately reigns supreme.

PRINCIPLE #5 IT'S OK TO BE DIFFERENT.

You'll begin to build your own market when you construct a clear ideology and push it out into the world. Despite the fact that not everyone will agree with you, if 1,000 individuals feel strongly about it, you have 1,000 potential customers. If you don't know why you're doing what you're doing, you'll become just another commodity in the throng.

"Warren Buffet has a philosophy when it comes to investing. Oprah has a philosophy on television content. Richard Branson has a philosophy when it comes to building his team and his brand. Elon Musk has a philosophy about why it's important to go to other planets."

It's okay to fail. Remember Twitter's popular 'fail whale'. Does it make you want to use them less though? Maybe, but for the majority, it's strangely not. The failed whale signaled to the market that the platform was in such great demand that almost everyone wanted to use it. In short, Twitter was oversubscribed.

"Tell people there's a problem caused by too much demand. Let them know you're working on having it fixed as soon as you can and they should try again soon."

Finally, it's okay to buck the trend. If everyone in your industry charges by the hour, try selling at a fixed cost. If everyone else sells components, sell bundles. If everyone is showing off their heritage, be a thought leader and a disruptive brand.

PRINCIPLE #6 VALUE IS CREATED IN THE 'ECOSYSTEM'.

Don't be afraid of giving away ideas. Focus on charging for implementation. If you're a yoga apparel brand, consider building a blog or social media profile where your market can read, listen to or watch free tutorials. Better yet, you can even invite them to a free yoga class.

"In the information age, you must remain conscious of the value shift from information into implementation."

Over the years, LEGO has extended their brand and partnered with others in highly innovative ways. But one thing they stay true is their 'brick system'. It's the core of who they're and they know not to mess with it. Expectant mums and dads all over the world look forward to playing with LEGO bricks when their child is old enough. Where would the magic be if LEGO decided to take away that tradition to welcome a new toy in a world of rapid change?

"Innovate but don't mess with a winning formula."

PRINCIPLE #7 NOTHING BEATS BEING POSITIVELY REMARKABLE.

Cut your marketing budget. Replace it with a remarkable budget. Imagine an electronics company takes out an ad that says "Take Amazing Photos with our New DSLR!". You read the ad and remember holiday season is around the corner. Your next move is to splash out on advertising and instead, open a browser and start looking at DSLR reviews. The company paid advertising fees to get you consider their DSLR but it ended up driving sales to the other companies. Daniel suggests you take at least fifty percent of your marketing budget and transfer it to a 'remarkable' budget.

"Being remarkable is not about offering stupid gimmicks or pointless stunts. It's about being the best in your niche or micro-niche."

Gone are the days when a company of any size could survive as a faceless corporation that exists as a set of logos, colors, symbols and sounds. Today, people want to know who the founder is, the CEO's background and what sort of beliefs the founding team holds. Companies that become oversubscribed leverage the personal brands of the people inside the organization.

11 Build-Ups to Being Oversubscribed

1. Signal the power (use the power of authority)
2. Name your terms (be willing to disqualify prospects and fire bad customers)
3. Don't ask for the sale (ask for the signal of purchase)
4. Be transparent

5. Think mobile and media first (harness the power of visuals and simplicity)

6. Educate and entertain (if your focus is on education, throw in a bit of entertainment too, and vice versa)

7. Wait for 7-hour before you talk business (Japanese businessmen rarely talk business until after a round of glass or two. It can actually blow the deal to bring up the topic of business too soon.)

8. Be visible offline and online (brains can hardly tell it's digital).

9. Start at the end (build products for prospects, not the other way around).

10. Under promise and overdeliver (keep quiet about some of the good stuff you know you can deliver).

11. Up your energy (enthusiasm and excitement drive loyalty, trust, connection and purchase decisions more than anything else).

12/15 – Giving Your Client the VIP Treatment (High End Coaching)

High-end consulting, if done right, is exactly how you WILL become a millionaire with your expertise. This stream of income is about attracting clients who are willing to pay a significant sum of money in exchange for the outcome you provide. For example, I provide high-level consulting, that can cost anywhere from $25K to $55K, depending on the qualifications of the client. That said, I always guarantee that whoever makes the investment will at least triple their money, which means that if someone pays $25,000 and follows my instructions to the letter, they will at least make $75,000. That's because my high-end consulting has never had any clients who didn't make at least six figures. That assurance and value that I provide are a win-win for everyone involved.

Consider, however, this; for those who provide high-end consulting, you are telling the person you are working with: Give me this money and, based on what I am going to teach you, I will increase your wealth three times over. So, if you're selling anything for $25,000, it should be at least worth $75K or $100,000 in results for your client. If you get 40 people to agree to your $25,000 program, you've made $1 million. This could be done in a year, in 6 months, in 90 Days, in a Month, and even in one day! This all depends on your process and capacity.

It's all about determining what the end result is that you can get for that individual. In some cases, you may have to turn down clients to maintain the integrity of your coaching. That's why my recommendation for anyone who wants to begin offering high-end consulting is to have an application procedure in place rather than just allowing anyone to pay. That way, you're screening your potential clients. ONLY take on as many clients that you can actually provide results for in order to keep your word and reputation in tact!

Below is an example of my high-end consulting questions. Click the link below and go through the questionnaire but DO NOT hit submit unless you are serious about joining my program:

https://www.mastermindwithash.com/apply1

13/15 - Guarantee That Others are Successful (Masterminds)

As Napoleon Hill put it, "Two or more persons, who labor toward a particular goal, in the spirit of harmony, "is called a mastermind! A mastermind group is one of the best things you can do for your message and your brand because you are able to spread your message based on results not based on advertising or sales. What I mean is that masterminds are meant for high level people who already believe in your message but just need help implementing it, so you don't have to convince them about your philosophy. Also, because they are high level people, they are willing to pay a premium for fast results which will in turn give you the social proof and word of mouth that you need in order to attract other high level likeminded people. Masterminds can cost over $100,000+ per person per year but the return on investment is always between 5-10X. Several of my books have inspired me to start mastermind groups, one of which is centered on teaching people how to live a life of Abundance and 10X their business. It's called the Abundance Community Inner Circle.

Keep in mind that a mastermind group is not the same as high-end consulting, although you can combine them as a bonus. High-end consulting allows you to work directly with the client instead of the group setting that mastermind programs provide.

For a high-end consulting program, you're working with the client one-on-one, and they're getting your undivided attention.

A Mastermind, on the other hand, is a group of likeminded individuals coming together to learn from each other. You act as the facilitator and host but still provide an outcome and environment for participants to obtain an increase their investment.

A mastermind program can help you take your main philosophy in your book and expound it into high level thinking that will benefit your participant on an exponential level. Below are the necessary steps in creating your program:

THE MASTERMIND GROUP LAUNCH CHECKLIST

PART 1 – THE BASICS

1.	Decide on your format. Will it be online or offline?
2.	How long will each person's session last? This will determine how many people you can have in your group. Ensure you give them enough time (minimum 20 minutes, maximum 90 minutes). Allow for five minutes to wrap each session and five-minute comfort breaks between each session.
3.	Once you know how many people you can have in your group, you can then get to the fun part. How many people can you have in your group? Once you know this, you can then see:
4.	How much will you charge for each member, and how much in additional monthly income will this mean for you/ your business?

THE MASTERMIND GROUP LAUNCH CHECKLIST

PART 2 – THE LAUNCH PROCESS

1. Decide on your cut-off date for applications. This should be two to four weeks from when you announce the launch of your group, which will give you enough time to send your email sequence.
2. Draft your emails leading up to the deadline.
3. Each email should end with a link to apply to join your Mastermind Group, where potential members set out why they want to join.
4. Have vetting calls with all who complete the application form to see if they will be a good fit for your group.
5. Send terms and conditions (min 6/12 months) and Direct Debit payment link to secure place (consider reductions for 12 months payment in advance– much better as fully bought in - and charge a premium for paying monthly). Ensure that it stipulates they must attend 80% plus of meetings.

6. Once accepted into group – schedule 1:1 to drill down into where they are now, have they been stuck for a while, what is their biggest challenge that they want this Mastermind to achieve for them for the year etc – this is the pain that you will hold them accountable to and come back to and you will use to show them how much the Mastermind has helped them.

7. Only send dates once everyone in the group has confrmed – it is impossible toplease all attendees.

THE MASTERMIND GROUP LAUNCH CHECKLIST

PART 3 – THE DAY

1. Welcome everyone to your group and outline the day ahead and time frames.
2. Show them the order of play – who goes when.
3. Explain your rules (eg outline their challenges for 5/10 minutes, 15 minutes of questions then summarise/agree actions). Make a note of the highlight for each person. If there is not an obvious one, ask them for their personal highlight at the end of their session (useful for later).
4. Make a note of who promises to do what by when (for the next session).
5. Close the day, but highlight each person's biggest breakthrough (to remind them of the value from the day).

THE MASTERMIND GROUP LAUNCH CHECKLIST

PART 4 – AFTER THE MEETING

1.	Encourage communication within the group outside of mastermind days
2.	Give your group access to learning material that they can learn and implement on their own
3.	Openly reward group members who reach or exceed a predetermined outcome to encourage others in the group to keep going but also to give them something to brag about outside of the group and possibly attract new members in the group
4.	Plan team building activities and retreats to give added value and encourage lifelong subscriptions

14/15 – Going Farther Together (Joint Ventures)

There's an African Proverb that says, "If you want to go fast, go alone, but if you want to go far, then go together." Joint Ventures or JVs are one of the best and fastest ways for you to make a lot of money and a lot of impact!

In my nearly 20 years as an author and publisher, I've seen how books open doors to new relationships. A well-written, professionally published, and expertly marketed book gives you instant credibility and accelerates collaboration. Influencers want to partner with you because you're now an expert in your subject matter. Books create bridges to greater trust and partnership

A joint venture involves two or more businesses pooling their resources and expertise to achieve a particular goal. The risks and rewards of the enterprise are also shared.

The reasons behind forming a joint venture include business expansion, development of new products, or moving into new markets.

Entering a joint venture is a major decision. This guide provides an overview of the main ways in which you can set up a joint venture, the advantages and disadvantages of doing so, how to assess if you are ready to commit, what to look for in a joint venture partner and how to make it work.

The worksheet below will give you a step-by-step guide on what to look for when creating a joint venture:

Types of Joint Ventures

The way you set up your Joint Venture (JV) will all be determined by what you aim to accomplish with the partnership. In some cases, it may be to work with another company or influencer in a limited capacity. For example, a company or influencer that has a unique and intriguing product, but a small network would connect with another company or influencer to sell it through a larger distribution network. A great example of this is Ciroc which is NOT owned by Sean Combs, aka P Diddy. Ciroc has a unique product, and Sean Combs has a large network as well as marketing tactics, so they partner to grow the brand. A contract could be drawn up between the two parties outlining the terms and circumstances of this arrangement.

Alternatively, two entities can decide to come together to create a new firm or a distinct joint venture to handle all business pertaining to the partnership. With a joint venture corporation like this, you can have a lot of control over your business. As a result, all of the partners have an equal stake in the company's success.

The third option can be that two businesses entirely merge to form a new entity that is co-owned by the respective parties. Before you enter into this type of JV, think about whether or not you want to be involved in the management of the new company. Also, consider what could happen if the company goes awry and how much risk you're willing to take in order to make an informed decision.

It's a good idea to seek legal guidance in order to choose the best course of action. Setting up your joint venture in a specific method might have a significant impact on its management and taxation. If the enterprise goes awry, your liabilities will also be affected. You must have a written agreement outlining the terms of the partnership and how any profits will be split.

Benefits and Risks of Joint Ventures

JVs can be used to strengthen long-term partnerships or collaborate on short-term projects, depending on the needs. Getting access to new markets and distribution networks through a successful JV is possible, especially to share the risks and costs with your JV partner. A JV can also be quite flexible in its approach. With a short life span and limited coverage, JVs limit both the commitment of both parties and the vulnerability of the business.

JVs can also come with some dangers or risks. The process of partnering with another company might be difficult. The right partnership takes time and works to develop.

Problems are likely to arise if the following conditions are met:

- There is a disparity in the levels of expertise, investment, and assets brought into the venture by the various partners.
- There is poor integration and cooperation due to different cultures and management styles.
- The partners do not provide sufficient leadership and support in the early stages.
- The partners have a different vision for the joint venture.

Research and analysis of goals and objectives are critical to a JV's success. Effective communication of the business plan is imperative.

DOES A JOINT VENTURE MAKE SENSE?

Establishing a joint venture can reflect a major shift in your company, so problems are likely to develop. No matter how valuable it is to your company's future growth, it must be integrated into your entire business strategy. Before agreeing to a joint venture, it is essential to assess your business plan. This will help you understand what to expect. Perhaps there are better ways of accomplishing your business goals.

It's also a good idea to have a peek at what other businesses in your industry are doing. As a business owner, it may be helpful to see how other companies or influencers have used joint ventures in the past. While you're doing it, you may try to figure out what abilities they use to work well together. You can improve your business by looking at it from a different perspective. Do some SWOT analysis to see if the two companies are a suitable fit for each other. Be honest with yourself about your strengths and limitations. In most cases, you'll want to select a joint venture partner that can balance out your company's positive and negative aspects.

CREATE A JOINT VENTURE AGREEMENT

Once you've determined that a Joint Venture is a good idea, it's time to put everything down on paper. Once the joint venture is fully up and running, this will help avoid any misunderstandings.

Your JV written agreement should include:

- The way the JV will be structured; IE: short-term relationship, separate businesses, new entity, or merger
- What the JV looks to accomplish
- The amount of money each partner will contribute
- Whether any existing assets will be transferred into the JV
- Who's going to own the Intellectual property created by the JV
- Standard Operation Procedures or S.O.P
- How debts and profits will be managed
- What is the arbitration process and how will disagreement be handled
- An exit strategy if the JV is no longer working

To secure any proprietary secrets you reveal, you may additionally require other agreements, such as a confidentiality agreement or a non-disclosure agreement better known as an NDA.

Before making any final decisions, it is imperative that you seek the advice of an attorney or impartial expert. The foundation of any successful partnership is a well-articulated understanding of each other's expectations.

Consider the following suggestions:

- Set a positive tone for your relationship right from the start.
- Communication is a crucial aspect of creating the partnership so scheduling regular face-to-face meetings for all essential members of the joint venture is usually a smart idea.

- Sharing financial information freely also helps partners avoid suspicion each other. The more trust there is in your relationship, the more likely it is that it will succeed.

ENDING A JOINT VENTURE

Even if a partnership can evolve with the times, it's certain to come to an end at some point. You can't expect your joint venture to continue once the project is completed if it was set up to do so.

It is often easier to end a joint venture if you have already dealt with the most important difficulties. It is possible for a joint venture to contain termination provisions. For instance, you might be entitled to quit the arrangement with three months' notice from each of you individually. Depending on the terms of the initial agreement, one partner may be required to buy out the other.

As part of the original agreement, it is important to lay out what will happen when the joint venture is terminated. For instance: how will the joint venture's intellectual property be broken up? How will confidential information be protected? Who will be entitled to any future income from the joint venture's activities? Who will be liable for any ongoing liabilities, such as debts and guarantees given to customers?

A well-thought-out agreement is not guaranteed to be free of problems. For instance, you may have to decide who will continue to handle a certain customer. If you plan ahead and take a constructive stance in negotiations, you'll be able to come to an amicable agreement. As a result, there's a better chance you and your partner will be able to work together in the future. It can also help you gain a reputation as a trust-worthy and effective business partner.

15/15 – Sharing the Wealth with Others (Affiliate)

Having a book published is a great way to get the word out about your business to other professionals in your field and those who will naturally gravitate towards your business. When they find your book and create value from it, they will easily spread the word to their friends, family, and colleagues.

When they do, it's a good idea to thank them with a commission from your affiliate program. People love to spread the word about businesses that provide excellent products and services. They appreciate it much more if they get paid for their efforts.

Creating an affiliate program allows you to formally pay them for their efforts while simultaneously creating a marketing machine that will get you paid over and over and over again. Passive income is the holy grail of online and offline business, the dream every entrepreneur chases. But passive income isn't just one plan or income stream. It's made up of several different types of cash flowing into your business, and one of the most popular is affiliate sales

To learn how to properly execute all of the above make sure you check out **BookRichUniversity.com** or use our software at **BookRich.io**

CHAPTER IV

Marketing and Promotion

Marketing and promotion are important aspects of self-publishing. Without a proper marketing strategy, it can be difficult to get your book noticed and attract readers. Some ways to market and promote your book include:

- Utilizing social media to reach potential readers and create buzz about your book
- Building an email list to connect with readers and promote your book
- Offering giveaways and discounts to attract readers
- Creating a book trailer or other video content to showcase your book
- Reaching out to book bloggers and reviewers for reviews and exposure
- Participating in online book communities and groups
- Utilizing paid advertising on platforms like Facebook, Instagram, and Amazon

- Building a strong author website and blog
- Creating an author brand and engaging with readers through webinars, podcasts, or other events
- Collaborating with other authors, influencers, and businesses to cross-promote each other's work
- Offering your book as a free or discounted book in exchange for reviews
- Utilizing existing platforms like Goodreads and Bookbub to advertise your book.

Marketing and promotion take time, effort, and a bit of creative thinking but it is worth it to reach a wider readership and build a fanbase.

BUILDING A MARKETING PLAN

Building a marketing plan is an important step in promoting your book. A marketing plan will help you identify your target audience, set goals and objectives, and develop strategies to reach those goals. Here are some steps to help you build a marketing plan for your self-published book:

1. Identify your target audience: Who are the readers most likely to be interested in your book? What are their demographics, interests, and reading habits?
2. Set your goals and objectives: What do you want to achieve with your marketing plan? Some examples may include increasing book sales, building an email list, or growing your social media following.
3. Develop strategies: Once you have identified your target audience and set your goals, it's time to develop strategies to reach

them. Some strategies may include utilizing social media, building an email list, offering giveaways and discounts, or participating in online book communities.

4. Allocate a budget: Determine how much you can afford to spend on marketing and allocate your budget accordingly. Some marketing efforts are low-cost or free while others require more investment.

5. Create a content calendar: Plan out your marketing efforts in advance. This will help you stay organized and make the most of your marketing efforts.

6. Measure your results: Keep track of your progress by monitoring your website analytics, social media metrics, and book sales. Use this data to adjust your marketing plan as needed.

7. Continuously evaluate and adapt your marketing plan: Your marketing plan should be a living document that you can continuously update and adapt as you learn more about your audience, your book, and the market.

By following these steps, you can create a comprehensive marketing plan that will help you effectively promote your self-published book.

Utilizing Social Media

Social media is a powerful tool for self-published authors to connect with readers, build an audience, and promote their books. Here are some ways to utilize social media to promote your book:

1. Create a social media presence: Set up accounts on major social media platforms such as Facebook, Instagram, Twitter, and Goodreads. Make sure your profile is complete and professional and include links to your website and book.

2. Build a community: Engage with your followers by posting regular updates, responding to comments, and sharing relevant content. Use hashtags to connect with other authors and readers in your genre.

3. Use visuals: Share eye-catching images and graphics related to your book, such as book covers, excerpts, and behind-the-scenes content. Use video content like book trailers, author interviews, and reading from your book.

4. Run contests and giveaways: Use social media to run contests and giveaways to increase engagement and attract new followers.

5. Share reviews and testimonials: Share positive reviews and testimonials from readers and influencers to build credibility and attract new readers.

6. Utilize paid advertising: Utilize social media advertising to reach a wider audience and promote your book to potential readers.

7. Utilize author-specific platforms: Utilize author-specific platforms like Bookbub, Library Thing, and Goodreads to connect with readers and promote your book.

8. Collaborate with other authors: Collaborate with other authors in your genre to cross-promote each other's books and expand your reach.

By utilizing social media effectively, you can connect with readers, build a community, and promote your book to a wider audience.

NETWORKING AND PARTNERSHIPS

Networking and partnerships are an essential part of building a successful self-publishing career. Here are some ways to build relationships and partnerships that can help promote your book:

1. Attend book events: Attend book fairs, festivals, and conferences to meet other authors, publishers, and industry professionals. These events provide opportunities to network, learn about the industry, and promote your book.

2. Join writing groups and organizations: Join writing groups and organizations that align with your genre or interests. These groups provide opportunities to connect with other authors and learn about opportunities for promotion and collaboration.

3. Reach out to influencers: Identify influencers in your genre or niche and reach out to them to see if they would be interested in reviewing or promoting your book.

4. Connect with local bookstores: Connect with local bookstores and libraries to see if they would be interested in hosting book signings or other events to promote your book.

5. Collaborate with other authors: Collaborate with other authors in your genre to cross-promote each other's books, co-write a book, or even create a box set together.

6. Utilize your existing network: Utilize your existing network of friends, family, and colleagues to promote your book. Ask them to share information about your book on their social media, leave reviews and tell others about it.

7. Partner with online platforms: Partner with online platforms like Amazon or Goodreads to promote your book and reach a wider audience.

Networking and partnerships can help you build relationships and expand your reach as a self-published author. By building connections and partnerships, you can promote your book to a wider audience and position yourself for success in the self-publishing industry.

BOOK LAUNCHES AND EVENTS

Book launches and events are an important part of promoting a new book. Here are some tips for planning and executing a successful book launch:

1. Plan ahead: Plan your book launch at least a few months in advance. This will give you enough time to organize the event, promote it, and build buzz.
2. Choose the right venue: Choose a venue that is appropriate for your book and your audience. Consider factors like location, size, and ambiance when selecting a venue.
3. Invite your audience: Invite your readers, fans, friends, family and other relevant people to your book launch. Use email, social media, and other marketing channels to spread the word.
4. Make it interactive: Make your book launch interactive and engaging. Consider incorporating activities like book readings, Q&A sessions, or book signing sessions.

5. Use social media: Use social media to promote your book launch. Create a hashtag, live-stream the event, and share photos and videos to build buzz.

6. Utilize influencers: Reach out to influencers in your genre or niche and ask them to attend or promote your book launch.

7. Follow up: After your book launch, be sure to follow up with attendees and thank them for coming. Use the momentum of your book launch to continue promoting your book and building your audience.

Book launches and events are a great way to promote your book and build buzz. By planning ahead, choosing the right venue, and making the event interactive and engaging, you can create a memorable experience for your readers and position your book for success.

CHAPTER V

SCALING YOUR SUCCESS

S caling your success as a self-published author involves finding ways to increase your income, reach more readers, and expand your business. Here are some tips for scaling your success:

1. Write more books: The more books you have available, the more opportunities you have to make sales and reach new readers. Consider writing a series or creating a collection of short stories or novellas.

2. Diversify your income streams: Look for new ways to monetize your book and your platform, such as offering coaching, consulting, or speaking services.

3. Expand your reach: Use social media, email marketing, and other tools to connect with new readers and expand your audience.

4. Leverage your book for other opportunities: Use your book as a stepping stone to other opportunities, such as speaking engagements, podcast appearances, or other forms of media coverage.

5. Create a community: Build a community of loyal readers and fans who will support your work and promote it to others.

6. Collaborate with other authors and industry professionals: Collaborate with other authors and industry professionals to increase your exposure and reach new audiences.

7. Invest in your business: Invest in tools and resources that will help you grow your business, such as a professional editor, book designer, or marketing expert.

8. Continuously improve: Continuously improve your writing and your business skills to stay ahead of the competition and position yourself for long-term success.

Scaling your success as a self-published author requires a combination of creativity, hard work, and strategic thinking. By focusing on writing more books, diversifying your income streams, expanding your reach, and investing in your business, you can position yourself for long-term success as a self-published author.

WRITING MULTIPLE BOOKS

Writing multiple books is an important strategy for scaling your success as a self-published author. Here are some tips for writing multiple books:

1. Plan ahead: Before you begin writing, plan out your book series or ideas for future books. This will help you stay organized and ensure that your books are interconnected and build on each other.

2. Set a schedule: Create a schedule for writing your books and stick to it. This will help you stay on track and ensure that you are able to write multiple books in a timely manner.

3. Write in batches: Instead of writing one book at a time, try writing multiple books at the same time. This will help you stay motivated and keep your writing momentum going.

4. Reuse and recycle: Reuse and recycle elements from your previous books to save time and effort. For example, use characters, settings, or plotlines from previous books in your new books.

5. Collaborate: Collaborate with other authors to write a series of books together. This can save time and effort, and also help you reach new readers.

6. Outline: Outline your books before you start writing them. This will help you stay on track, and save you time and effort.

7. Hire a team: Hire a team of professionals to help you write multiple books. This could include editors, proofreaders, and book designers.

Writing multiple books is a great way to increase your income and reach new readers. By planning ahead, setting a schedule, and reusing and recycling elements from your previous books, you can write multiple books efficiently and effectively.

BUILDING A BRAND

Building a brand is an important aspect of scaling your success as a self-published author. Here are some tips for building a brand:

1. Define your brand: Before you start building your brand, define what it is and what it stands for. This will help you create a consistent message and image for your brand.

2. Create a consistent aesthetic: Use the same colors, fonts, and imagery across all of your marketing materials to create a consistent aesthetic for your brand.

3. Establish a voice: Develop a consistent voice for your brand that reflects your personality and values.

4. Be authentic: Be true to yourself and your brand. Your readers will appreciate honesty and authenticity.

5. Be consistent: Consistency is key when building a brand. Be consistent in your messaging, your aesthetic, and your voice.

6. Use social media: Use social media to build relationships with your readers and promote your brand.

7. Build a website: Build a website that represents your brand and provides a platform for readers to connect with you and learn more about your books.

8. Network and collaborate: Network with other authors, bloggers, and influencers in your genre to collaborate and promote each other's brands.

9. Engage with your readers: Respond to comments and messages from your readers, and engage with them in a way that aligns with your brand.

By creating a consistent aesthetic, establishing a voice, and engaging with your readers, you can build a brand that resonates with your audience and sets you apart as an author.

Outsourcing and Delegation

Outsourcing and delegation are key strategies for scaling your success as a self-published author. Here are some tips for outsourcing and delegation:

1. Identify your strengths and weaknesses: Determine which tasks you are best at and which tasks you struggle with. Focus on outsourcing or delegating the tasks that you struggle with or don't enjoy.

2. Hire a virtual assistant: Consider hiring a virtual assistant to help with tasks such as bookkeeping, scheduling, and social media management.

3. Utilize freelancers: Freelancers can be a great resource for tasks such as editing, cover design, and formatting.

4. Use outsourcing platforms: Platforms like Upwork and Fiverr can be great resources for finding freelancers for various tasks.

5. Set clear expectations: When outsourcing or delegating, make sure to set clear expectations for the task, the deadline, and the desired outcome.

6. Communicate effectively: Maintain open communication with your outsourcing partners to ensure the work is done to your satisfaction.

7. Prioritize tasks: Prioritize the tasks you need to outsource or delegate in order of importance so you can focus on the most critical ones first.

8. Build relationships: Build relationships with your outsourcing partners and freelancers so you can continue to work together in the future.

By outsourcing and delegating tasks that you struggle with or don't enjoy, you can free up your time to focus on the aspects of your business that you excel at and enjoy.

Another part of outsourcing and delegating is using funnels, upsells and down sells, email sequences, and SMS text to automate your book sales.

Funnels: A marketing funnel is a series of steps that a potential customer goes through in order to purchase your book. The top of the funnel is where you attract potential customers with content, such as blog posts, videos, and social media posts. As they move through the funnel, they are presented with different offers, such as a free chapter of your book or a discounted copy. The goal of the funnel is to lead them to purchase your book.

Upsells and Downsells: Once a customer has purchased your book, you can use upsells and downsells to increase revenue. An upsell is when you offer a related product or service at a higher price, such as a course or coaching package. A downsell is when you offer a related product or service at a lower price, such as an ebook or audiobook.

Email Sequences: Email sequences are a series of automated emails that are sent to a customer at specific intervals. You can use email sequences to nurture your relationship with your audience, provide valuable content, and promote your book.

SMS: SMS (short message service) is a text messaging service that can be used to communicate with your audience. You can use SMS to send promotions, updates, and reminders about your book.

By using these techniques, you can establish yourself as an authority and thought leader in your niche, while also automating your book sales. This will allow you to focus on creating valuable content and building relationships with your audience.

To learn how to properly execute all of the above make sure you check out **BookRichUniversity.com** or use our software at **BookRich.io**

Staying Current in the Industry

Staying current in the self-publishing industry is essential for continued success as an author. Here are some tips for staying current:

1. Read industry blogs and publications: Stay up to date with the latest trends, news, and tips by reading industry blogs and publications such as The Independent Author Network, The Creative Penn, and Self-Publishing School.
2. Attend conferences and events: Attend conferences and events to network with other authors and industry professionals, learn new strategies, and stay current on the latest industry trends.
3. Join online communities: Join online communities such as BookRichUniversity.com, Facebook groups and online forums to stay connected with other authors and learn from their experiences.

4. Listen to podcasts: Podcasts are a great way to stay current on the latest industry trends and gain insight from successful authors and industry professionals.
5. Participate in webinars: Participate in webinars to learn new strategies and tactics, and stay current on industry trends.
6. Keep up with technology: Stay current with technology, and tools such as book marketing software and new e-book formats.
7. Create a Learning Mindset: Continual learning is essential in any profession, and authorship is no exception. Keep a learning mindset and be open to new ideas and ways of doing things.

By staying current in the industry, you can stay ahead of the curve and continue to grow your business and succeed as a self-published author.

CHAPTER VI

CONCLUSION

I n conclusion, self-publishing is a viable option for authors looking to take control of their career and build a fortune as a self-published author. By understanding the business side of self-publishing, crafting a compelling book idea, and utilizing various monetization strategies, you can create multiple streams of income from your book. Additionally, building a platform and audience, and utilizing marketing and promotion strategies can help you reach a wider audience and increase your book sales. It is also important to stay current in the industry, by keeping up with the latest trends and technology, participating in events and communities, and being open to new ideas and ways of doing things. Following the steps outlined in this book, you can be on your way to creating a successful and profitable career as a self-published author.

Self-publishing can be a challenging but rewarding journey. It takes hard work, dedication and a lot of effort to become a successful self-published author. But it is not impossible. Many successful authors have taken the self-publishing route, and you can too. You have the knowledge and the tools to make your dream a reality. Don't let fear or doubt hold you back. Take action now, and start working on your book today. Remember, the best time to start was yesterday, the second-best time is now. Don't wait any longer, start creating your legacy today.

ADDITIONAL RESOURCES FOR FURTHER LEARNING

If you appreciate simplicity and want to get up and running with your book business, I recommend joining **BookRich.io,** it is a powerful platform that simplifies the process of managing your book business by consolidating all the necessary tools in one place. As a self-published author, you can use **BookRich.io** to create sales funnels, automate email sequences, manage SMS messaging, and handle your social media all in one place. This eliminates the need to use multiple technologies and makes it easier for you to run your book business, saving you time and energy. Additionally, by using **BookRich.io**, you can easily scale your income and grow your business exponentially. The platform's automation and integration capabilities allow you to streamline your sales and marketing efforts, which can ultimately lead to increased revenue and success as a self-published author.

BookRich.io can help self-published authors by providing a platform for them to easily create and manage their sales funnels, email sequences, and SMS campaigns. This can help authors automate their book sales and increase their revenue. Additionally, **BookRich.io** offers a variety of tools and resources to help authors build their brand and establish themselves as thought leaders in their industry. These tools include webinar platforms, membership sites, and affiliate management. **BookRich.io** can also provide authors with access to a community of other authors and experts who can offer support and guidance as they navigate the self-publishing industry. Overall, **BookRich.io** can provide self-published authors with the tools and resources they need to build a successful business around their book and establish themselves as a thought leader in their field.

Some other helpful resources include:

1. Self-Publishing School - An online course that teaches you how to write, publish, and market your book.
2. The Creative Penn - A website that offers resources and tips for self-publishing authors.
3. The Self-Publishing Podcast - A podcast that provides in-depth interviews and advice on all aspects of self-publishing.
4. The Alliance of Independent Authors - An organization that offers resources, events, and a supportive community for self-publishing authors.
5. The Book Designer - A website that offers tips and templates for formatting and designing your book.
6. Amazon Kindle Direct Publishing - Amazon's self-publishing platform that allows you to upload and sell your book on Amazon.
7. Kobo Writing Life - Kobo's self-publishing platform that allows you to publish and sell your book on Kobo.
8. Barnes & Noble Press - Barnes & Noble's self-publishing platform that allows you to publish and sell your book on Barnes & Noble.

These resources can provide valuable information and support as you navigate the self-publishing journey. Be sure to take advantage of them as you work on your book.

ABOUT THE AUTHOR

Ash Cash Exantus is a renowned financial educator and motivational speaker who has dedicated his career to teaching financial literacy, wealth building, and entrepreneurship. He uses a culturally responsive approach in his teachings, making financial concepts accessible and relatable to a diverse range of audiences.

Dubbed the Financial Motivator, Ash has a proven track record of success, having authored four bestselling books, with a total of 13 books published. He is the CEO of 1BrickPublishing, a company that helps entrepreneurs add six-figures or more to their business by leveraging the power of a book, even if they don't write it themselves.

In addition to his own successful publishing and business ventures, Ash also helps other authors become leading authorities in their field through his expertise and guidance. With his wealth of knowledge and experience, Ash is well-equipped to empower individuals and entrepreneurs to take control of their finances and achieve their goals.

He is also the Founder of **BookRich.io**, which is an all-in-one platform that helps authors streamline their business operations and create multiple streams of income. It allows authors to manage their funnels, email sequences, SMS campaigns, and social media in one place, which makes it easy to grow their income exponentially. With **BookRich.io**, authors can create upsells and down sells, automate their book sales, and build their brand and authority as a thought leader in their field. Additionally, it can help authors with their book publishing and distribution, as well as monetizing their book in various ways. Overall, **BookRich.io** is a powerful tool for authors looking to take their book business to the next level and create multiple streams of income.